The British Horse Society

Career Pathways

Complete Horsemanship
Volume I

Supporting you through every stage

The British Horse Society

Career Pathways

Complete Horsemanship
Volume I

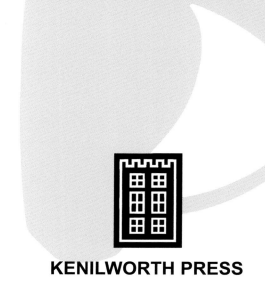

KENILWORTH PRESS

Acknowledgements

The British Horse Society would like to thank all those who have been involved
in the development and production of *Complete Horsemanship Volume I* including
Berkshire Riding Centre, Home Farm Hothorpe, Millfield School, Warwickshire College,
Wellington Riding Centre, The BHS Quality and Training Committee,
Cardboard Bedding Solutions Ltd, Jon Stroud Media, Sorbeo Horse Bedding,
Tara Taylor Photography, Lucy Higginson and Sabrina Jones FBHS.

First published in the UK in 2017 by Kenilworth Press,
an imprint of Quiller Publishing Ltd

Reprinted 2018, 2020

British Library Cataloguing-in-Publication Data
A catalogue record for this book is available from the British Library

ISBN 978 1 910016 16 9

Edited by Martin Diggle
Design by Arabella Ainslie

Printed in Wales

Kenilworth Press
An imprint of Quiller Publishing Ltd
Wykey House, Wykey, Shrewsbury SY4 1JA
Tel: 01939 261616
Email: info@quillerbooks.com
Website: www.kenilworthpress.co.uk

Contents

Introduction

Introduction

Welcome to the *Complete Horsemanship* series from the British Horse Society (BHS). If you are passionate about horses and want to learn more about how to care for them and improve your riding skills, this first volume is for you.

In it you will find chapters on how to:

- Understand why horses behave the way they do and how to handle their behaviour.

- Feed, groom, and generally look after horses.

- Recognise what to look for on a day-to-day basis and know who to tell if you think a particular horse is unwell or behaving differently.

- Describe and talk about the physical make-up of horses.

- Understand what horses need on a daily basis.

- Tack up and provide rugs for horses doing different types of work.

Most of all, it will help you have fun developing your riding and horse management skills, whether you want to enjoy this wonderful sport recreationally, or you're thinking about pursuing a career with horses.

If you are thinking of a career in the equestrian world — whether as a groom, equine dentist or physiotherapist, or even if you aspire to riding in the Olympics, you will need to develop the skills that will make you stand out to employers.

The BHS education system is one of the best and most widely-respected in the world. The *Complete Horsemanship* series supports anyone wishing to study qualifications within the BHS Career Pathway. There are a number of bespoke professional career pathways available, depending on your long-term goal. Whether it's becoming a successful groom or a stable manager, an equine teacher or a specialist coach, there's a pathway to choose from.

Equestrian qualifications show potential employers the skills accrued for a career with horses. The BHS qualifications framework is internationally recognised, with some of the best instructors, riders and grooms coming through the BHS Career Pathway, including Fellows Carl Hester and Yogi Breisner. The BHS Career Pathway gives each student the opportunity to gain qualifications and awards in their chosen profession. They have been specially developed through extensive consultation with the equine industry to incorporate the latest research and thinking, with current practices and friendly assessment methods.

Complete Horsemanship

SECTION I
CARE

The British Horse Society

Career Pathways

Chapter 1

Horse Behaviour

Evolution, domestication and 'flight or fight'

Herd life

Summary

Evolution, domestication and 'flight or fight'

If we are to understand why horses behave the way they do, we first need to learn the behaviour of wild horses and how domestication has led them to adapt to a changed environment. Horses have been domesticated for around 6,000 years and their interaction with humans has given them the benefits of regular food, water, treatment of disease and injury and protection from predators. However, with domestication comes behavioural changes — a domesticated environment can be very unnatural. A wild horse is able to choose his herd mates, may browse for his own food and water and is free to choose how and when he socialises, exercises and rests.

A domesticated horse is often stabled, restricting in his freedom to move, browse for food or water, or socialise and interact with other horses.

Horses have evolved over millions of years to browse and eat for 14–16 hours per day and can travel huge distances in the wild in search of food and water. They are also prey animals and have depended on their flight or fight instinct for survival. When frightened, they will usually run away, but if this isn't an option they may fight.

Although horses in our care face far fewer threats, their flight or fight instincts still lead them to run first and think later; they may often spook at things that humans are unable to see, hear or smell.

Herd life

Horses are very social, herd-orientated animals and are very good at communicating, cooperating and looking after one another. They form close relationships with one another and often create friendships called pair bonds, which can last a lifetime. These relationships help keep them safe from predators, as herd members can keep an eye out for one another and raise the alarm if they see a threat. Even in a domesticated herd you will rarely see all the horses lying down together; instead herd members take turns to rest while another horse stands over them as a lookout.

Many of us have experienced a horse who calls and paces the fence line when left in the field on his own, or one who refuses to load, naps when leaving the yard on his own, or doesn't seem to be able to concentrate during a dressage test.

Some horses suffer from separation anxiety, becoming very stressed when away from other horses, and must be gradually re-educated to feel safe when alone. The same is true for horses who barge out of the stable in the morning in anticipation of being led to the field, or become excited and jog on the way there. Escaping the confines of the stable for the exercise, social interaction and grazing available in the field can be very exciting.

Horses in a herd.

You may have heard people talk about 'alpha' mares or stallions, by which we refer to horses who appear to be in charge of the others and will fight off those who stand in their way.

Different horses lead the herd in different situations — one particular horse or pair may lead it in search of better grazing, for example — but you may see a different horse 'taking charge' of a pile of hay and yet another one seeing off a predator to protect the herd.

Social interaction and structure

To create a peaceful and safe herd, it is important to establish social structure; however, this structure is very complex. Many people believe it is constant and based on dominance, which is not always the case. Although you may see a horse being aggressive towards another in a domesticated environment, this is because resources such as food, water and space are limited and the horse exerts aggression to secure enough to eat. For example, you may see one horse fighting off the others when hay is put in the field. However, such behaviour may be far less common in the wild if resources are plentiful. Similarly, you may see a domesticated horse show territorial aggression to a field mate who comes too close, but compare the space a horse has in the wild to that available in a small man-made paddock. The domesticated horse is simply using his survival instinct to ensure he has enough food and space. You will often see that horses grazing together will establish a 'pecking order', on the basis of who is the most dominant animal.

Dominant horse sending another horse away.

Horses may also be territorial in the stable, perhaps turning their hindquarters threateningly towards an approaching handler. They may also lunge at another horse walking past their stable in an attempt to defend their space.

The frustrations of confinement can sometimes be expressed through territorial aggression; entering a stable you might be greeted with laid-back ears and bared teeth, or a horse might kick the stable wall when eating. Try to turn out a horse who does this as much as possible and, if he has to be stabled, ensure that he has plenty of forage and stable enrichment such as toys. Other manifestations of such emotions are biting the stable door, the lead rope or even themselves. A horse may also be protective of his food; perhaps he has been bullied in the field or was starved in the past. Remember that aggression is rarely seen in wild horses and the way we look after and manage our horses will shape how they behave.

An aggressive horse may be very dangerous and some such behaviour becomes habitual and difficult to change.

If a horse is showing aggressive behaviour it is important to ask a vet to check whether there are any physical issues (e.g. back or teeth problems) underpinning the behaviour. Ill-fitting tack can be a trigger, so you need to seek advice if you think this might be a problem.

Having forage available at all times helps decrease anxiety and territorial behaviour about food: remember in the wild horses would eat for 14–16 hours a day. See if any horses in the field are showing aggression, and consider whether they have enough space, enough food to eat and enough water.

Horses cannot talk but they communicate with us through their body language and facial expressions, sometimes coupling the latter with movement. A horse may put his ears back if another horse comes too close. If the intruder continues to approach, the horse who feels his space is being invaded may then lunge forward, baring his teeth threateningly.

Like humans, every horse is an individual and will show different behaviour when stressed, anxious or threatened, and it is important to understand how each one expresses his emotions. Some horses may be anxious, neighing, pawing at the ground and moving around the stable if a new horse joins the yard, while others may quietly eat from their haynet.

A relaxed horse.

As we said earlier, the flight or fight instinct may help protect horses in the wild, but running away can be a bad idea in domesticated situations. We therefore need to help horses become more confident to help prevent them from spooking, which can be dangerous for their riders and handlers.

Facial features and expressions

Eyes

As a prey animal, horses have large eyes and rely on their eyes and wide field of vision to watch out for predators. Horses have 215-degree vision but cannot see directly behind or directly in front of them, which means you should take care to avoid alarming them when walking behind them. Horses can tell the difference between blue and green in bright conditions but they struggle to distinguish colour in dim light. They may find it more difficult to jump if an obstacle is the same or close to the colour of the ground. Also, horses find it more difficult to judge a fence if it is painted in a single colour (e.g. white wings with white poles) than if the fence is painted in two different colours (such as blue and white poles).

They find it difficult to adjust their vision when moving from a bright area to a dark one, and may find this frightening, e.g. a dark stable or trailer. When a horse is scared you may see the whites of his eyes. This can also indicate aggression, in which case you should remain calm and assess whether it is safe to approach.

Ears

Horses cannot hear low sound frequencies well but their ability to hear high ones is very advanced. This means they can hear and locate sounds such as a twig snapping, which humans may easily miss. The ears are a great indicator of where the horse's attention lies and how he is feeling. A horse with pricked ears is often alert, interested and listening to something in front of him. If the ears are back, he may be listening to something behind him. If the horse is frightened or aggressive then the ears may be pinned backwards against the head. Ears held to the side often indicate that the horse is relaxed, and they may flick back and forth as the horse listens to the rider.

Nose and mouth

A horse's sense of taste and smell are very important in investigating new objects, working out what is safe to eat, and are also involved in how horses greet and socialise with one another. A horse may flare his nostrils and snort when he is frightened, or the nostrils may narrow and you will see wrinkles when he is annoyed or irritated.

A horse may also curl his top lip and show his teeth, which may make him look as if he is laughing! This is called the Flehmen response and is usually seen when a horse smells or tastes something unusual or unfamiliar. A horse may also show his teeth when he is annoyed but this is usually paired with pinned-back ears. The mouth will often be tense and tight when the horse is worried or annoyed, but relaxed when calm and content.

Body language

As discussed above, horses use their whole bodies to communicate with one another, and learning what to watch out for when a horse is telling you he is anxious, stressed or about to kick, bite or spook will help you to keep safe.

When resting or dozing, horses may also rest a hind leg, droop their bottom lip and close their eyes. However, when a horse is uptight, sees something he perceives as a potential threat or may be about to spook, the head and neck are raised, the ears snap forward towards the object of their attention, the muscles become tense, the tail is raised and the nostrils flared.

This horse's facial expression warns you that he is not happy.

Head and neck position

A raised head and neck may suggest something the horse perceives as a potential threat has caught his attention — he may be about to spook at something in the hedgerow, for example. But the head and neck may also be raised when the horse is being ridden, indicating that the horse does not understand the rider's aids, is in pain, or is avoiding the bit. Conversely, a resting horse will often have a low head and neck, but this could also suggest illness or depression. It is very important to look at the whole body, posture and facial expression to tell.

Tail

The tail position also tells you a lot about how a horse is feeling. If it is clamped down, the horse may be worried or anxious. Slow swishing may be to get rid of flies, but may also denote anxiety. An aggressive or irritated horse may swish his tail from side to side quickly; this could also indicate that he is about to kick or bite. A raised tail may indicate that something has caught the horse's attention. Remember the flight or fight instinct that the horse has? Biting and kicking derives from the fight aspect; if horses feel cornered and are unable to escape something frightening they may lash out.

Summary

- A wild horse has a very different life from a domesticated one but they share the same needs: the company of other horses, forage and freedom to exercise.

- Wild horses eat for 14–16 hours per day and walk many miles to search for food and water. Domesticated horses still have a great need to exercise and eat for many hours per day.

- Horses have a hard-wired run now, think later flight or fight instinct and often spook at things we cannot see, hear or smell. When horses spook or run away this is simply a response to their survival mechanism. In a horse's mind, they need to run away in order to survive.

- Domestication has changed the way a horse behaves as a consequence of the unnatural environment we put our horses in. How we stable, ride and feed them from haynets is very different from a wild horse's lifestyle.

- Horses love to socialise with other horses in a herd environment and some may be anxious when taken away from other horses or kept on their own.

- Pecking order and aggression may develop between horses in a domesticated herd environment.

- Horses show aggression for a variety of reasons. For example, they may put their ears flat back and bare their teeth if another horse gets too close to the hay they are eating in the field, or they may lunge out when another horse walks past their stable in an attempt to defend their space.

- An aggressive horse may be very dangerous. This behaviour can be very difficult to change as it will often have been caused by a past event, which can be self-reinforcing and become a habit.

- Horses communicate with us through their body language and facial expressions.

- To keep safe around horses you must be able to read a horse's body language and facial expressions to understand how he is feeling and how he is going to react.

TRAINING TIPS

1. Spend time observing horses in their stables or out in their fields to see how they interact with others.

2. Watch how horses interact with people.

3. Observe the facial expressions and body language of the horse while you are working with him, and how these change with different situations.

Chapter 2

Safety around Horses

Safety around Horses

Safety: it's a word that makes people roll their eyes. However, it is crucial to understand why it is so important around horses, and how you as an individual play a part in it. The easiest way to stay safe is to pay careful attention to everything you do, and consider beforehand, 'What could go wrong?' (this is sometimes called a risk assessment), so that we all can reduce the chance of those things happening. An employer has a legal responsibility to ensure that an employee's health, safety and welfare are protected (Health and Safety at Work Act 1974). However, legally, an employee also has to take necessary precautions, such as wearing personal protective equipment (PPE), attending training and following any safety rules put in place by management. You have a responsibility to yourself, your colleagues and your employer (as well as to the horses) to work in a safe and responsible manner. You must also tell your supervisor or employer about any potential health and safety issues you are concerned about.

When handled badly, horses have a well-documented potential to bite at one end and kick at the other. Their behaviour, while perfectly normal to them, may be unexpected to us. Therefore you can never absolutely predict what a horse is going to do. By learning as much as you can about equine behaviour, you can be better prepared for most situations; prevention really is the key. You may lead the same quiet and easy horse to the field every day for a month without issue; then one day something unexpected could result in rope-burnt hands if you haven't worn gloves, or — more seriously — a major head injury if you are not wearing your hard hat. Even the best, most experienced horse people get it wrong from time to time.

Looking after yourself

Working on a yard is physically demanding and often requires you to think on your feet. On a busy day we are all guilty of improvising with whatever comes to hand rather than sourcing the correct tool for the job. However a one-off improvisation may quickly become a habit that may cause problems at another time.

Hopefully, carrying out a 'dynamic' (on the spot) risk assessment is something you do automatically. It simply means that you consider the possible consequences before tackling a task. Never feel you must do something in a certain way just because it has always been done in that way. Ultimately it is you who could end up hurt. If you can see a potential risk you MUST make people aware and find a safer way to do it. Often it is just a case of using common sense.

Pay attention to what is happening around you. If someone is trying to lead an excitable horse out to the field, hopefully you will recognise how unpopular you will be if you choose this moment to trot another horse down the yard or shake a rug out. Make sure you communicate clearly to help protect each other's safety. At most yards the practice of stopping before entering an arena and calling out to anyone inside for permission to enter is used. This gives the riders inside time to adjust their speed, location, or to let an inexperienced horse see that the door is open. In return, it may save you from getting run over the moment you step inside.

Having music in the yard can create a good atmosphere, but make sure you can hear each other in case someone needs help or a loose horse suddenly clatters in. Similarly, it is safer not to use headphones.

PPE — vital safety kit

Wearing PPE (personal protective equipment) should be part of your everyday routine. It is sometimes seen as an inconvenience, but simple measures such as keeping a pair of gloves tucked in the waistband of your jodhpurs so they are accessible may save your hands from injury. While it is not necessary to wear a hat all the time, it is sensible to put one on (and fasten the chinstrap) when leading, riding or lungeing horses, or in any situation where you may be vulnerable, no matter how quiet the horse is perceived to be. A frightened horse can lash out in a split second and catch your head accidentally, with life-changing consequences.

What you wear on the yard might not seem important, but being comfortable and correctly dressed for the job reinforces your professionalism. As country folk have a habit of telling you, there is no such thing as the wrong weather, only the wrong clothes for the weather. Make sure you are prepared for all eventualities; there really is nothing worse than being soaked first thing in the morning and having to stay wet or cold all day.

You can never guarantee how a horse is going to react when turned out; a correctly fitted hat and gloves are essential items of PPE in this situation.

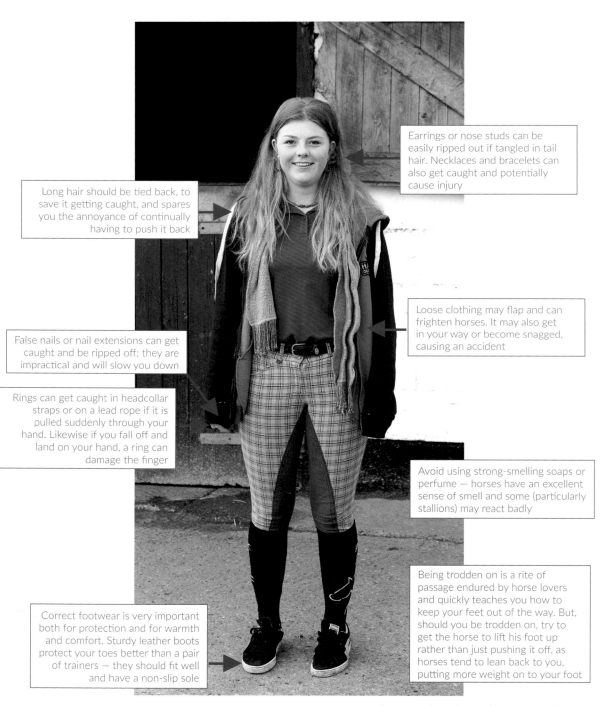

Earrings or nose studs can be easily ripped out if tangled in tail hair. Necklaces and bracelets can also get caught and potentially cause injury

Long hair should be tied back, to save it getting caught, and spares you the annoyance of continually having to push it back

Loose clothing may flap and can frighten horses. It may also get in your way or become snagged, causing an accident

False nails or nail extensions can get caught and be ripped off; they are impractical and will slow you down

Rings can get caught in headcollar straps or on a lead rope if it is pulled suddenly through your hand. Likewise if you fall off and land on your hand, a ring can damage the finger

Avoid using strong-smelling soaps or perfume — horses have an excellent sense of smell and some (particularly stallions) may react badly

Being trodden on is a rite of passage endured by horse lovers and quickly teaches you how to keep your feet out of the way. But, should you be trodden on, try to get the horse to lift his foot up rather than just pushing it off, as horses tend to lean back to you, putting more weight on to your foot

Correct footwear is very important both for protection and for warmth and comfort. Sturdy leather boots protect your toes better than a pair of trainers — they should fit well and have a non-slip sole

Incorrect dress for working on a yard.

In the summer it may be tempting to top up your tan in a vest top, but this leaves vulnerable areas such as the tops of your arms and collarbones exposed. A T-shirt offers an extra layer between your skin and the floor, and an uneven tan is a small price to pay for life-limiting wounds, bites or grazes.

Manual handling

Good lifting technique is often overlooked. The damage inflicted from bad technique often accumulates, giving you a problem some time later. It may be more convenient to carry one water bucket but this doesn't do your back many favours. Split your load between two buckets and carry one in each hand. Partially filled buckets are less likely to spill and the load will be equally balanced. To resist strain when lifting, you should bend your knees and keep your back straight; it might seem awkward at first but you will soon get used to it. If you have heavy or clumsy things such as bags of feed to move, use a wheelbarrow. If there is anything you can't comfortably lift on your own, ask for help. Both lifters should bend their knees, keep a straight back and make sure they lift at the same time.

Physical fitness

Working with horses is physically demanding. If you are unused to this sort of work, you may find it takes time to get 'yard fit', and that you lag behind completing tasks and feel tired sooner than your workmates.

Just as you wouldn't tackle a half marathon without training for it, you need to build up progressively the amount you do on the yard to avoid overloading your muscles and joints. You must also be willing to push yourself through this stage, as it will get easier over time.

Avoiding injury when handling horses

Horses are, by nature, unpredictable and, in certain circumstances, even the quietest horse may act unexpectedly. Observe the horse's body language and facial expressions and take steps to keep both of you safe. Consider what may have caused the horse to react and whether there are steps you could take to avoid a recurrence. If a particular horse gives indications that he may be difficult to handle — biting, kicking or becoming unsettled in the field or stable — report it to your supervisor without delay. Such behaviour may compromise the horse's welfare and your safety.

Some common situations include:

1. **A horse who kicks or tries to nip when being groomed or tacked up**

   This often results from the horse being uncomfortable or very sensitive to touch. The answer is to find a way to work with the horse rather than rebuke him. Always tie the horse up in a way that gives you plenty of room to move around him without becoming trapped against a wall. Try to stand close to the quarters when grooming so, if the horse does kick, you are pushed out of the way rather than on the receiving end of a full body blow. Take care when brushing around sensitive areas (e.g. under belly, stifle, girth area) and use firm strokes with a soft brush to try to avoid accidental tickling. Fastening the girth is likely to provoke a reaction from a sensitive or uncomfortable horse, so fasten it slowly and gently. If you are dealing with a horse known to react badly to girthing (e.g. by cow-kicking), it may be prudent to wear a hard hat when bending down to take the girth under his belly.

2. **A horse who becomes unsettled when you enter the stable or field**

Try to work out what has upset the horse. It may be better to give the horse time to settle before going closer, rather than provoking further upset; for example, if the hunt has just passed by. If the horse becomes restless because he cannot see others, moving him may help him to settle again. Always think about your own safety first.

Accident procedure

Make sure you know the names of your yard first aiders and the location of the first aid kit. Attending a first aid course is an excellent idea.

If you do come across an accident:

- Stay calm and assess the situation. Do not put yourself in danger; if you get hurt you can't help anyone.

- Make the area safe. If there are loose horses they could cause further injuries to the casualty and to you.

- Get help.

- Encourage the casualty to keep still and reassure them.

- Keep them warm with a coat or blanket.

- Follow instructions of the person in charge. You may have to phone for an ambulance so make sure you know the yard's postcode and give clear details of where the accident is. You might be asked to stand at the entrance to the yard to direct the ambulance.

- You might be required to sign the accident book as a witness.

Defining accidents and incidents

Accidents, or situations that might cause an accident in the workplace, must be recorded by law to help your employer and co-workers take steps to prevent future ones.

An *accident* is something that results in someone being injured or falling ill (e.g. a fall from a horse, a crushed foot when a horse steps on it).

An *incident* is a near miss, undesired circumstance or a dangerous occurrence.

A *near miss* is a term used to describe something that does not harm anyone, but may have the potential to injure someone or make them ill (e.g. stacking shavings bales incorrectly — even if they don't hit you they may land on someone else at some stage).

Undesired circumstances are usually conditions that could cause injury or ill health (e.g. someone being asked to do something they don't understand or have not been trained to do). If this happens to you, you must speak up.

Dangerous occurrences have high potential to cause death or serious injury. A list of examples is found in 'Reporting of Injuries, Diseases and Dangerous Occurrences Regulations 2013 (RIDDOR)' (e.g. explosions, electrical incidents, lifting, machinery failing).

Fire precautions

Every yard owner dreads a fire; it can sweep rapidly through hay and bedding. Every yard should have someone responsible for organising fire precautions that includes clear signage,

It is important to be familiar with the location of fire-fighting equipment and associated procedures.

fire extinguishers in suitable locations, planning evacuation routes for humans and horses and ensuring these routes are kept clear. Take the time to look around the yard and make sure you are familiar with these routes and know where the fire extinguishers or hose pipes are. A senior member of staff should take you through the fire procedure when you start work. If they don't, make sure that you ask them to.

An example of a fire procedure might be:

- Raise the alarm by shouting or setting off the alarm.

- Alert a senior staff member.

- Phone the fire brigade (if asked to) — make sure you know the postcode of the yard and any directions they may need to reach you.

- Follow instructions from a senior member of staff — this may include moving horses from stables to designated fields.

- Go to the assembly point.

- Human safety must be put above horse safety — even if you find this upsetting.

Insurance

Although this will be covered by an employer in most cases, it is a good idea to check that you are insured while you are riding and working. If you are a freelance worker, insurance is essential for your own protection. Public Liability cover is important if you have an accident that involves a third party or damages someone's property (such as the horse you are riding kicking a parked car). Personal Accident cover is also strongly recommended, especially if you work on a freelance basis. If you are unable to work because of an injury, consider how you will cover your living expenses.

BHS gold membership provides some insurance cover but you may wish to top this up through a specialist insurer. Make sure you read any small print and take the time to compare policies to ensure you have the cover you need.

Summary

- Be aware of your responsibilities for keeping yourself and others safe at work.

- Take steps to look after yourself, such as wearing PPE and the correct clothing.

- Pay attention to what is going on around you.

- Risk assess dynamically.

- Use safe lifting techniques — you only have one back!

- Make sure you are familiar with the fire and accident procedures on your yard.

- Always report accidents or incidents.

- Investigate insurance to protect yourself.

- Think about your own fitness; look after yourself.

TRAINING TIPS

1. When you have quiet time, walk around the yard and look at it thoroughly. Try to imagine all things that could go wrong or cause a problem, then think how you might avoid these.

2. Every time you have a near miss or you see or hear of someone else having one, make sure you learn from it. Why did it happen? What can you do to prevent it from happening again?

Chapter 3

Handling Horses

Handling Horses

Spending time handling different horses gives you a great opportunity to get to know their personalities. As with people, there will be some you will get on with better than others but you will need to learn how to work with them all. Watching and working with different horses will build the valuable skill of recognising what behaviour is normal for each horse and more importantly, what it is not, however subtle the signs may be.

Pay attention to how the horse reacts when you first approach the stable. Some are naturally protective of their body space and may pull a face to warn you off; others may enjoy you being there, or not even register you. Think about your body language as you approach the horse. Try to be quiet but positive in your body language and voice, no matter what kind of mood you are in. This will give the horse confidence in you and therefore more likely to be more accepting of you. Try to put any frustrations to one side. Even if you are upset about something, or you are running late, if you let that translate into tense body language the horse will instantly be on his guard.

Speak to the horse as you approach to get his attention before you open his stable door. If you know the horse is quiet, a gentle rub on the forehead or neck can be a great ice-breaker. While you are doing this, cast your eye over the horse and ask yourself if everything looks okay. Is the horse standing normally; has the feed been eaten; are there normal droppings; does the horse look comfortable? If the answer to any of your questions is 'no', you may need to investigate further or ask for advice. It need only take a few seconds but it's an excellent habit to form, and it's something most top riders and grooms do instinctively every time they first see a horse in the morning.

If the horse is standing very close to the stable door and this makes it hard for you to go in safely, put your hand on his chest and say 'back', giving a little push. Most well-trained horses will step back, allowing you to enter the stable and shut the door behind you. A horse who likes to push his way out may need to be moved back from the door before you open it (reach over the door and push the horse back with your hand, using a confident voice at the same time). When the horse moves back, go in and shut the door quickly, not forgetting to shut the top bolt. Once in the stable, ask the horse to move back again to give you space to work. Don't let yourself get stuck between the door and the horse; always try to stay to the side of the horse, especially if you know he can be pushy.

Securing a horse in the stable

Putting on a headcollar

Put the lead rope around the horse's neck so you have control if he sticks his head up and moves away from the headcollar when you try to put it on. Some horses move around in the stable, which may make things a bit harder. By having the lead rope around the horse's neck you can keep hold of both ends, stay at the shoulder and follow the horse round, so you still have control, but the horse has time to relax. Remember, when a horse does something like this it is often because of a previous bad experience or underlying tension. Most horses stop when they realise you are in control. If the horse is really not happy to stand to have the headcollar put on, taking a treat, such as a carrot, mint or handful of nuts, in with you can help distract him long enough to get the job done. Bribery is not something you should rely on regularly though; it is better to have help to retrain the horse to respond correctly.

A correctly fitted headcollar.

Putting on a headcollar will become an easy task with practice, but always remember that the horse's comfort should be the priority. The headcollar should fit the horse's head and not rub the bony areas, with the noseband above the fleshy part of the nostrils, having enough room to fit three fingers all the way around. Standing to the left of the horse when putting on a headcollar is a good idea as standing in front could result in being headbutted should the horse throw his head up.

Putting the headcollar strap over the top of the horse's head, behind the ears, can cause issues for both horse and handler, especially if the horse is taller than you. Sliding the strap behind the ears and down the other side is far less startling for the horse than if you flick the strap over and catch it.

Tying up a horse

Horses should always be tied to something that will break easily if they panic and pull back. Without that, they can hurt themselves, and you, badly. It can be a very frightening situation when a horse really panics. Horses are flight animals and do not like to feel restricted. If a horse can't break free he may damage his head and neck or break the headcollar.

This is easily avoided by attaching string to a tie-up ring with which to tie the horse. If it's broken or missing, you can replace it with a reasonable length of baling twine. If you ever have to tie a horse up to thick string and you cannot remove it to make it thinner, separate several strands from the loop and tie the rope to the thinner piece instead.

There are two methods of tying a quick-release knot. Both are fine to use and which one you use will come down to your own preference, but every rider and groom should know one. The horse should not be tied up so tightly that you cannot position him where you want him to stand — any tighter than this and the horse may feel too restricted and pull backwards. On the other hand, if horses have too much freedom you may find they move around too much.

Method one:

i. Place the end of the lead rope through the tie-string and cross it over the rope to create a loop.

ii. With the free end of the rope, make another loop and thread it through.

iii. Make another loop with the free end of the rope and thread it through the middle of the previous loop.

iv. You can thread the tail of the rope through the final loop to stop the horse from undoing the knot if he plays with the rope.

Method two:

i. Make a loop about two-thirds of the way down the lead rope from the clip.

ii. Thread the loop through the tie-string.

iii. Make a loop with the free end of the rope and thread it through the previous one, pulling the knot tight.

iv. Then thread the tail through the loop to stop the horse undoing it.

Picture sequences of how to tie quick-release knots

A horse tied with a suitable length of lead rope. To release the horse, simply unthread the tail and pull firmly down.

Cross-tying

This is a method of securing the horse up with a rope from either side of his headcollar, so he is unable to swing his head round completely one way or the other.

When you tie up your horse like this, make sure that you leave enough space either side of him so that you can work safely without being squashed and that both ropes are tied to pieces of string as mentioned above.

Leading a horse

You will probably do this every day, if not several times a day. Normally you will lead from the left-hand side, but there are times when you may have to lead from the right (e.g. if you need to lead on the road in the UK). It is a good idea to practise this to make sure you and the horse are confident with it. Always wear a hard hat (do up the chinstrap) and wear gloves to give you a better grip (and to prevent rope-burn if the horse pulls the rope through your hand).

Once you are ready to take the horse out of the stable, open the door as wide as possible, hook it back if you can, then undo the lead rope, standing on the left side of the horse just in front of his shoulder. Put your right hand just below the clip under the horse's chin and take the end of the rope in your left hand. If the lead rope is long, fold it up across your hand to prevent it dragging on the floor or creating a loop in front of you that you might trip over. Winding the rope around your hand is unsafe; it may tighten around your fingers and can cause a bad injury or cause you to be dragged if a horse takes off. Lead the horse straight out of the middle of the doorway to reduce the risk of catching his hips on the door frame or the corner of the door. A horse who has had this misfortune in the past may try to rush through the doorway. In this case, you need to reassure him and work to gain his confidence. Make sure the horse is completely out of the door before turning, and remember to shut the stable door behind you. Some yards can be a bit slippery; try not to turn a shod horse too sharply.

Whether you are leading a horse to a field or to the arena to ride, the principles are the same. It is much easier to lead a horse who is walking actively forward and not needing to be encouraged every step of the way.

To give yourself the best chance of achieving this, and the most control, stand next to or slightly in front of the horse's shoulder, so you are in a position to encourage the horse forward or to slow

Allow the horse enough room when leading out of the stable.

down if required. This also allows you to read the horse's body language, react accordingly and control his shoulders when turning, reducing the risk of being stood on. Always pay attention to what is going on around you when leading, even if the horse is one you know very well and your route is one you take every day. Even the quietest of horses can sometimes perceive danger in the smallest changes and catch you by surprise.

If you come across something the horse is unsure of, like a plastic bag in a hedge, some horses may stop and lift their heads to stare at it and appear taller. Don't panic! Some will just have a look and a snort, then carry on. If not, stand up tall and try to keep yourself close to the horse's shoulder. Reassure him verbally and then ask him to walk on again, making sure you turn his head slightly away from the scary object to focus instead on you. He might scoot past it quickly, so stay positive and make sure you have a firm grip on the lead rope. A few little tugs down the lead rope might help to get the horse's attention back on you. Try not to be taken on an unplanned jog. If the offending object is on the right, be aware that the horse may step towards you or swing into you, so it might be safer to swap sides and then swap back again when the horse has settled.

Some horses can be quite keen and walk quickly, especially if they think they are going somewhere exciting. Try to keep up by walking a little bit faster yourself to match the horse, instead of pulling him back.

Leading the horse safely.

It is easy to get into the habit of walking in front of a lazy horse instead of leading him properly, but you have less control over a horse who is behind you: he could pull back and pull the rope out of your hand. You're also in a vulnerable position if the horse becomes spooked and jumps forward suddenly. Try to encourage an active walk by using your voice or clicking. Don't forget to praise the horse when he does get the hang of it. It can be hard work for him too, especially if he has always been allowed to dawdle.

Holding a horse for treatment or inspection

There will be many occasions when you will be required to hold a horse for someone: this might include holding him for the vet.

Some horses may be fine to handle in a headcollar, but for those you do not know very well, excitable horses, or ones who have spent time on box rest or may react to a wound being touched, a bridle is a good idea to give a little more control.

Your role as the handler is to keep everyone safe, even if the horse is having something out of the ordinary done to him and feels tense. As a handler you should be wearing gloves, sturdy non-slip boots and a hard hat.

Before bringing the horse out it is best to check that all the yard gates are closed in case the horse escapes, and check that the trot-up or inspection area is free from potential hazards. A nice flat area with a hard surface is ideal. One of your first challenges will be to get the horse standing as squarely as possible. Ask the horse to halt, and then if he is not standing square it is easier to make small adjustments by asking him to move backwards for a step or two until he is square instead of leading him forward. You might find this nearly impossible to achieve with some horses and, if the horse is in pain, it is far more important to let him stand comfortably than to force him into a square halt. Once the horse is standing how you want him, you should stand to the side of his head facing backwards so you can observe both his body language and the person working on the horse. If the horse is wearing a bridle you may want to take a rein in either hand to help keep his head straight. You can also reassure the horse from this position; sometimes a stroke down the neck is all that's required for a calm, quiet horse. If the horse won't stand still, use your voice confidently to tell him to 'stand'. A little pressure on the lead rope or reins may be needed too. Don't be tempted to position yourself directly in front of the horse to try to stop him; as you may get run over.

What do we mean by halting 'square'?

This means the horse is standing with his forefeet level with each other and the same with the hind feet. If they are not, then it is hard to compare both sides of the horse's body evenly.

Make sure you stand on the same side of the horse as the person treating it — if they are treating a cut or palpating a painful area, the horse may swing his quarters out or kick. At the same time, watch his facial expressions and warn the person if the ears go back, the horse rolls his eyes or threatens to kick (swishing tail, raising a hind leg). You can encourage the horse to stand quietly with a clear voice aid if required. If he tries to kick out or swing his quarters you must act quickly and pull the head and neck towards you, which swings the quarters away from you and the other person, so the horse should not be able to make contact.

Trotting up a horse

As part of a veterinary inspection you might need to lead the horse up in walk and trot, so the vet may assess how he moves and can identify any lameness.

This can be more difficult than it sounds, especially if the horse is lazy. Stay level with the horse's shoulder and focus on where you want to go, keeping the horse as straight as possible. Put your right hand towards the top of the rope or reins near the head but leave a little slack (around 30cm/1ft) otherwise you can restrict and alter the horse's movement. Have your left hand on the end of the reins or lead rope but make sure there is not much left dangling that you could trip over. Ask the horse to walk on, being positive with your voice and body language. The horse has to move forward without being dragged along behind you. If he is lazy you may want to carry a short whip. Hold the whip in your left hand and use it gently behind you towards the horse's quarters. This can act as a visual cue for acceleration rather than a reprimand. Once you have produced an active walk, slide your right hand further down the rein (about halfway down the rein or lead rope) so that the horse can move his head freely.

When turning the horse to come back again, slow down before the turn to avoid slipping. If the horse is very lame, make the turn wide and allow him to balance himself comfortably. Turn the horse by pushing his head away from you and staying next to his shoulder (you walk round the horse, not the other way round). This allows you to control the size of the turn and protects you from being stood on. Walk the horse in a straight line back again, remembering that some horses are keener on the way back so might be more active. Be ready to slide your right hand up the rein towards the chin again to help keep control.

To trot the horse in hand always start by walking him straight in an active walk before asking him to trot. A few clicks of encouragement can be helpful if the horse is not keen to pick up trot. Keep the rein short until you know the horse is under control and then let it gradually feed out of your right hand to allow the horse the freedom to move his head. This can be crucial if the horse is only very slightly lame and the vet needs to see every movement.

Turning the horse away from you to prevent you being stood on.

Bring the horse gradually down to walk before you attempt to turn, and make the turn wide enough for the horse to balance. Fully complete the turn and walk a couple of straight strides before you ask for trot again. As with the walk, some horses may be keener on the return trip, so be ready for a faster trot and try to keep the trot balanced, not rushed. The person observing will probably want to view the horse from the side, so be prepared to keep going past them for a few strides before gradually bringing the horse back down to walk.

It takes practice to be able to trot up a horse correctly and one of the hardest things is first to get the horse walking actively next to you. Get into the habit of encouraging every horse you lead to do so. This is can be a challenge with the more laid-back horse. Listen to how even the steps sound and how heavily the horse lands on each foot; each beat should be the same. Learning to recognise when it sounds different can help you spot a potential issue such as a loose shoe or a lame horse.

Handling horses in the field

Turning out

Going to the field can be the highlight of a horse's day. For this reason you should be safely dressed in a hat, gloves and boots. If the horse is known to be excitable you might want to put a bridle on for additional control. To make it easier and quicker to take off in the field, remove the noseband before you put the bridle on.

If there are several of you leading a group of horses to the field make sure one of you is in charge and tells the others when to do things. Lead the horses in single file with the stronger/more forward-going horses at the front and the more laid-back ones towards the rear. When you reach the gate make sure it is opened wide enough for the horses to get through safely: ideally have someone separate in charge of gates. If this person is holding a horse they should go into the field first, round the gate and stand on the other side of it facing back to the opening, so they can hold the gate without their horse getting in the way of the others coming through. The horses coming into the field should be led along the fence line and turned back to face the fence, making sure there is room between the fence and the horse for the handler to move away safely. From this position, if horses spin and buck when you let them go, they usually end up at least their own length from you before the hind legs come out.

Have someone in charge of counting down and let all the horses go at the same time, to stop any one horse from exciting the others before they are freed. As you undo the headcollar, step back from the horse in case he turns around and whips away. Don't turn your back on the horses as you move away; you need to see if they decide to come towards you. Don't be tempted to chase the horses away; this can encourage them to kick out and make it dangerous for the next person who turns that horse out. Let the horses move away in their own time.

When releasing a horse in the field, the horse should be turned to face the gate or fence and should be positioned with enough space for the handler to move away safely.

If you have led the horse out in a bridle, be careful taking it off so the bit doesn't bang uncomfortably on his teeth.

Some horses will put their heads down and eat straight away; others feel obliged to make several laps of the field first. Be careful as you make your way back to the gate in case the grazing horses suddenly decide to join in: it's easy for them to forget you are there and come crashing into you. It is a good idea to watch the horses for a few minutes to make sure they settle.

Catching

When catching a horse in from the field, approach his shoulder and make sure he has seen or heard you coming (remember horses have a blind spot right in front of and right behind them). Some horses may wander off and make things more difficult. You might have to follow them for a moment until they stand still, but make sure you walk to the side and not directly behind them. Sometimes a rustled bit of paper in your pocket can be enough to persuade them to stand (taking food into a field can be dangerous as you can end up with horses squabbling over it, so be careful if this approach is needed). In some circumstances you may need to take a titbit into the field but make sure you keep it in your pocket to prevent other horses from seeing it.

Some groups of horses like to have a final gallop around before they are caught. Make sure you are in a safe place and let them finish before trying to catch them; if you are lucky they might stop by the gate for you. Have the lead rope over your arm and the headcollar undone ready to put on. Once you have reached the horse you wish to bring in, give him a rub on the shoulder and place the lead rope over his neck. Once touched, most horses will stand still for you to put the headcollar on — but hold on to both ends of the lead rope around the neck in case you are dealing with the exception. Face forward and stand next to the horse's head as you put the headcollar on. You might want to put your arm gently around his nose to keep his head still.

Once you have adjusted the headcollar to fit, take the lead rope from around the horse's neck and lead him to the gate. Be aware of any other horses staying out in the field, as they might try to come out of the gate with you, or run around and excite the horse you are leading. Keep yourself in a safe position next to the horse's shoulder and be positive with the horse you are leading. Only open the gate as wide as you need to get the horse you are leading out safely. Ideally have a person in charge of the gate, and shut it securely behind you even if there are no horses left in the field. (Gates left open drop on their hinges and need repairing much more often.)

Summary

- Be safe — think about risk-assessing each situation for potential hazards. How might the horse react, why are you handling the horse, would it be safer to have a helper?

- Wear suitable PPE (hat, gloves and suitable footwear) when handling horses outside of stables.

- When tying up a horse, always make sure this is in a safe place.

- The lead rope should be tied to a piece of breakable string.

- Allow sufficient length of rope so the horse does not feel restricted, but not so much that there is a risk of him getting tangled up in it or putting his nose on the floor.

- Be aware of your body positioning next to the horse when leading. Make sure you are next to the horse's shoulder so you don't get stood on.

- Think about how your body language can affect the horse.

- Turning out or catching in are among the most dangerous tasks you will undertake.

- Horses can be more excitable going to the field.

- If possible, have someone to operate the gate to make getting horses in and out of the field easier.

- Be aware of everything happening around you, where all the horses are, what they are doing (grazing/galloping around?) especially if you are trying to take a horse away from the herd.

TRAINING TIPS

1. Try to accompany anyone turning out or catching in a horse or group of horses. Observe what they do, look for potential hazards and how the horses react to them; this will further your understanding of how horses behave and what type of things can cause them to react.

2. Observe horses on the yard and how they behave or react in different situations. It can be very interesting to see how horses have different reactions to the same thing.

3. Watch experienced handlers when they work around or handle tricky horses or youngsters. Observe their body language and how they interact with the horse and how he responds. Ask questions afterwards about what you saw.

4. If it is not going well and the horse is not doing what you want, question your actions before blaming the horse. Maybe you could ask in a different way? Ask for help or advice.

5. The more supervised practice you can do the better. Ask to be involved with trotting up horses for the vet or to help out with anything going on at the yard.

Chapter 4

Identifying Horses

Points of the horse

Anyone involved with horses benefits from learning how to identify their colour, type, breed, points (see below) and size. These skills are invaluable for checking that you are about to catch/ groom/tack up the correct horse, or for describing the site of an injury to an owner or vet.

If you are asked to catch in a bright bay horse, approximately 16hh, with two white socks on his forelegs and a star on his forehead you are more likely to be able to find that horse in a field full of bay horses than if someone said it's bay, average-sized and has some white markings. A knowledgeable description allows less room for error.

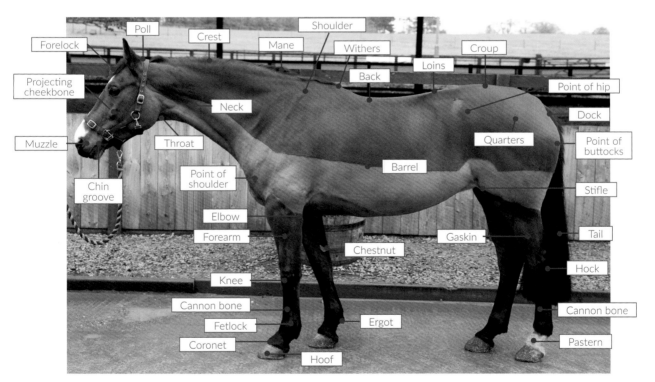

Points of the horse.

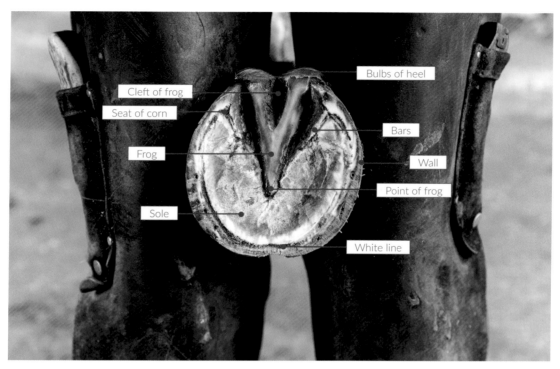

Cleft of frog

Seat of corn

Frog

Sole

Bulbs of heel

Bars

Wall

Point of frog

White line

Parts of the foot.

Colours and markings

Coat colour

A horse or pony's colour is defined not only by the actual coat colour but also by the colour of the 'points'. By this we mean the muzzle, the tips of the ears, the mane and tail, knees, hocks and the lower limbs. The points can be the same colour as the coat, or a different colour or shade. Coat colour is a fascinating subject and can be the subject of much debate. Breed societies have specific rules and definitions relating to colour, so make sure you check up on them if you plan to show under rules.

A black horse.

Bay horse with a brown coat with black points (can be classed as light, bright or dark depending on shade of coat colour). This picture shows a bright bay horse.

A chestnut horse is ginger or red in colour with the same coloured points, although they sometimes have flaxen manes and tails. A dark chestnut horse is called liver chestnut.

i. Grey.

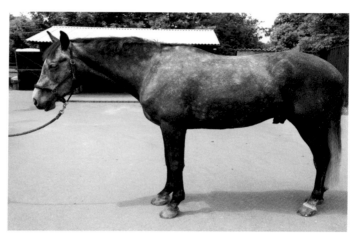

ii. Iron grey.

iii. Dapple grey.

iv. Flea-bitten grey.

Grey describes a horse with 'white' and black hairs throughout the coat. Since the term ' white' refers to a lack of pigmentation in the hair, it is not technically a colour and thus is not used to describe whole coat colour (although, for convenience, the term is used with reference to markings on the lower limbs, face, etc). Horses who appear white are almost invariably greys whose coat has lightened with age.

There are variations of grey: a 'dappled' grey appears to have circles or 'dapples' of a lighter or darker grey on the coat; 'flea-bitten' means there are dark-coloured tufts in the coat, giving the impression of dots or speckles; and an 'iron' grey is a very dark grey colour that may lighten as the horse grows older.

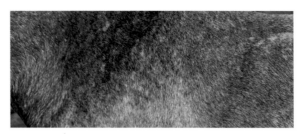

Strawberry roan. A roan has white hairs running through the coat, which can be chestnut (strawberry roan), bay (red roan) or dark bay, brown or black (blue roan).

A dun coat can vary from a dark 'mouse' colour to a golden yellow colour. The points will be black and there will be an 'eel' or dorsal stripe (a black line) running down the length of the spine. A horse of a similar colour without the dorsal stripe is not a true dun and is known as a buckskin.

A piebald coat involves irregular patches of black and white all over the body.

A skewbald has irregular patches of white and any other colour apart from black over the body.

A palomino is a yellow/golden colour coat that can vary in shade from light to dark. The mane and tail are white.

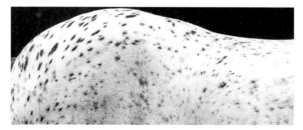

There are several different types of spot markings: 'leopard' spots describe spots of any colour on a light coat; 'blanket' spots are spots of any colour that cover a white rump; 'snowflake' spots are white spots on any colour coat.

Face and leg markings

As well as coat colour there are a variety of face and leg markings. It can be useful to describe these white markings (sometimes with black spots) on specific areas of the horse's face or legs in case you have to tell apart horses of a similar colour.

Facial markings

The white mark on the middle of the forehead is called a star.

A narrow white line running the length of the face staying within the width of the nose is a stripe. This horse has a star and stripe.

A blaze is similar to a stripe but wider and extends over the bones of the nose.

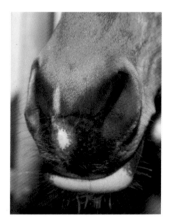

A snip is a white mark on the muzzle that is not attached to any other white marks on the face.

A white face is a marking that covers the forehead, eyes, nose and part of the muzzle.

Leg markings

Markings on the leg can be described using the part that they cover e.g. 'white pastern'. The more commonly referred to markings are the sock, stocking and ermine mark.

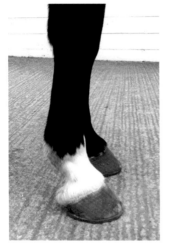

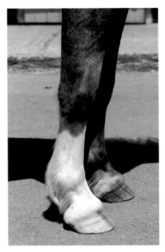

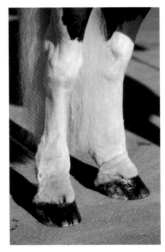

White to fetlock.

White to knee, also known as a sock.

White leg to above hock (or a stocking) with ermine marks. An ermine mark is a black spot.

How to estimate the height of a horse

Horses and ponies are traditionally measured in hands (hh) and sometimes now (especially by showing or breed societies, and in continental Europe) in centimetres. One hand is equal to 4in or just over 10cm.

The height of a horse or pony is measured from the floor to the highest part of the withers, with the results written as the number of hands and the remaining inches e.g. 12.1hh (or else entirely in centimetres). Very small ponies such as Shetlands may be measured in inches rather than hands. Any animal 14.2hh and under is classed as a pony and any animal above this height as a horse. Exceptions are polo ponies (this term is used regardless of size) and breeds such as the Falabella or Caspian — or miniature horses smaller than Shetlands, but as a breed still use the term 'horse'.

In most cases an approximate height measurement is acceptable when describing a horse, but there will be times when you require a definite measurement (e.g. to enter a height-specific showing class). It will help you to guesstimate the height of a horse if you know how tall you are in hands yourself. This way, when you stand next to the horse you have something with which to compare.

To take an accurate measurement of a horse's height, a measuring stick is used. This is a long ruler with the height in hands on one side and in inches or centimetres on the other. A shorter ruler with a spirit level sits at right angles to the main stick and is used flat over the horse's withers to obtain the height against the scale. Not all horses will be happy to be measured and some may tense up and unwittingly grow taller, whereas others may react by 'shrinking'. Wait for the horse to relax and stand naturally in order to get an accurate reading.

1. *Stand the horse square on a flat piece of ground.*

2. *Move the spirit level up to the top of the stick and place the stick next to the horse in line with the withers, making sure it is level.*

3. *Lower the spirit level until it sits on top of the withers.*

4. *Slide the stick sideways away from the horse and check the reading.*

It is becoming more common to see horses measured in centimetres, and this is the unit of choice on the continent and in showing or showjumping classes. It is helpful to learn some heights in centimetres so you have a rough idea what they are in hands.

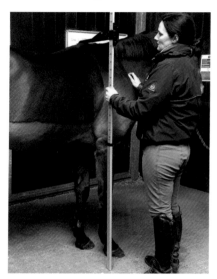

Measuring a horse's height.

Conversion chart: hands to inches and centimetres

Heights in hands	Heights in inches	Heights in centimetres (rounded to nearest cm)
13hh	52in	132cm
14hh	56in	142cm
14.2hh	58in	148cm
15hh	60in	152cm
16hh	64in	163cm
17hh	68in	173cm

Summary

- Learning the points of a horse will help you describe accurately where an injury or blemish is located.

- A horse's colour is defined by the colour of his coat, muzzle, mane, tail, knees, hocks and lower legs.

- A horse can have a variety of white markings on his face or legs, each with a specific descriptive name.

- The height of a horse or pony is usually measured in hands (hh).

- A pony is classed as anything under 14.2hh; a horse is anything over 14.2hh.

TRAINING TIPS

1. A good way to learn the points of the horse is to put an annotated poster on the wall somewhere you'll see it often.

2. Once you think you know them, a fun way to test yourself is to try putting sticky labels in the right place on a quiet horse or pony (taking care not to use anything too sticky that may cause irritation to the horse).

3. Practise describing different horses and ponies; the more you do it the easier it becomes if you are put on the spot.

4. Measure various parts of your own body in hands: the top of your head, your eyes, your chin and your shoulders are a good start. This gives you a reference point from which to calculate an approximate height. Try this out — then check against the horse's recorded height.

Chapter 5

Horse Health and Welfare

Signs of health

Owning or keeping a horse

Summary

Horse Health and Welfare

Caring for a horse, whether your own or someone else's, involves responsibility for his health and welfare. As every horse is slightly different, it's good to get to know what 'normal' constitutes for your particular horse(s), to help you spot any changes, however small, early. The sooner a problem is noticed and dealt with, the less likely it is to become more serious.

Any changes to the horse's normal behaviour should be reported to a senior staff member straight away, no matter how trivial it may appear. If in doubt, report it rather than ignore it. If you do not have the benefit of a more experienced colleague to refer to, or if the horse is your own, seek advice from your vet.

Signs of health

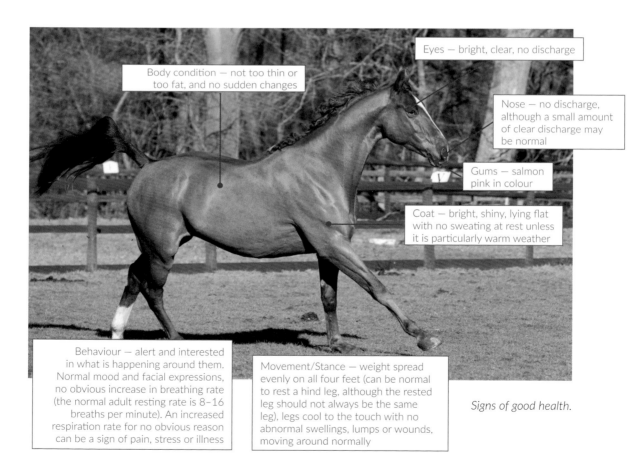

Body condition — not too thin or too fat, and no sudden changes

Eyes — bright, clear, no discharge

Nose — no discharge, although a small amount of clear discharge may be normal

Gums — salmon pink in colour

Coat — bright, shiny, lying flat with no sweating at rest unless it is particularly warm weather

Behaviour — alert and interested in what is happening around them. Normal mood and facial expressions, no obvious increase in breathing rate (the normal adult resting rate is 8–16 breaths per minute). An increased respiration rate for no obvious reason can be a sign of pain, stress or illness

Movement/Stance — weight spread evenly on all four feet (can be normal to rest a hind leg, although the rested leg should not always be the same leg), legs cool to the touch with no abnormal swellings, lumps or wounds, moving around normally

Signs of good health.

Droppings — passed regularly, normal amount, the colour and consistency may vary with the horse's diet but droppings should not be particularly hard or loose

Bedding — not excessively dug up or trampled

Urine — passed regularly, pale yellow or colourless, no foul smell

Appetite — drinking and eating a normal amount

A normal morning stable.

Routine checks

Monitoring the horse's health should be an integral part of your daily routine. It starts from the moment you arrive in the morning: eager heads may appear to enquire about breakfast — is any head missing that would normally be among them? If so, this may be a first indication of illness. As you walk down the yard, glance over stable doors to see if the horses are looking and behaving normally. Once in the stable, make a more thorough check; has feed and water been consumed in the expected quantities? Has the bedding been excessively disturbed; are there a normal number of droppings? You can also check the horse's general appearance, behaviour and stance, as well as running your hands and eyes over the body and legs for signs of swelling, lumps or wounds.

Such observations can continue whenever you are working around the horse in the stable or yard, or in the field. A second thorough check should be made towards the end of the day, perhaps in combination with evening stables. When you head for home at the day's end, the horses should be tucking into their hay, have plenty of water and be looking normal and relaxed.

Field-kept horses should be checked for general health, their feet picked out and rugs checked morning and evening. In between they can be more generally observed whenever anyone passes their field. Alongside the health checks, water, fencing and other field checks should also be made (see Chapter 10 Field Care).

Ill health

Signs may include:

- Head down or lack of interest in what is happening nearby.
- Standing away from the herd.
- Frequent rolling, turning the head towards the stomach or kicking up towards the stomach.
- Restlessness.
- Sweating at rest (on a cool day).
- Not grazing/eating (off food).
- Not drinking, or frequent drinking.
- No droppings or frequent, loose droppings,
- Urine dark in colour.
- Lying down for a long period.
- Reluctance to move, or lame.
- Resting a foreleg or pointing a foreleg.
- Very pale or very red gums.
- Dull, staring coat.
- Coughing.

The horse's body condition

After the general overview, there are some key areas to consider when assessing body condition:

- Crest.
- Over the ribs.
- Over the quarters.

Consider the horse from all angles to make a proper assessment. It is important to do this regularly and keep a record of the horse's body condition, particularly if there are several horses in your care. Any significant changes could indicate that the horse's feed is not adequate for their management and level of work, or that the horse has a serious illness.

Ideal body weight

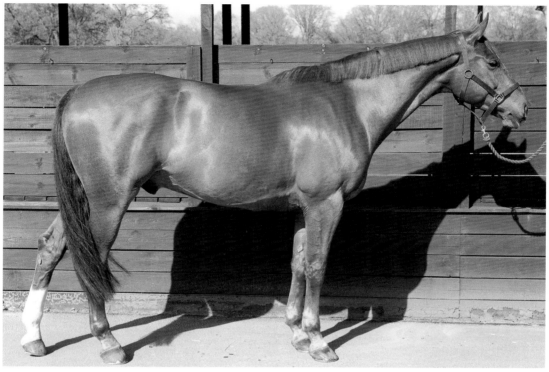

Ideal body weight. No noticeable crest (although some stallions may have a prominent crest). Ribs should be just covered and easily felt. No bones should be protruding.

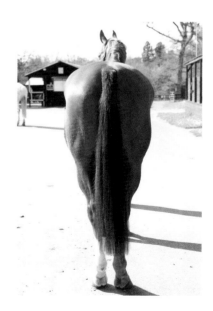

From behind there should be a rounded shape over the top of the quarters, with no channel down the spine. There shouldn't be any concavity on either side of quarters and the hip bones should not be protruding but should be easily felt.

Overweight

An overweight horse may show some or all of the following:

- Fat hump or solid fat stored at the crest.

- Ribs not tangible; fat deposits over and between the ribs.

- Fat deposits or excessive fat covering areas such as the shoulders, withers and neck.

- No definition of hips; fat stored either side of the spine creating a channel running down the spine.

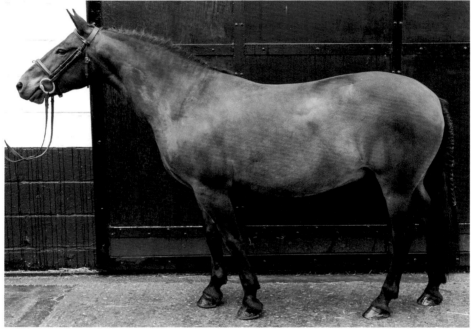

This horse has a fat hump at the crest and excessive fat stored on the neck, shoulders, withers and over the ribs.

Underweight

An underweight horse may show some or all of the following:

- Neck narrow with no fat covering.

- Spine, withers, shoulders and hip bones clearly visible and protruding.

- Ribs easily visible.

- From behind, the outline of the quarters is hollow and falling away.

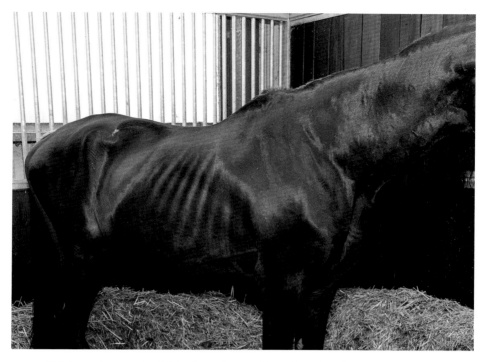

This horse has clearly visible ribs and protruding spine, shoulders, withers and hip bones.

Owning or keeping a horse

Welfare needs of the horse

Animal welfare acts require that any horse:

- Has a suitable environment to live in.
  - » Sufficient shelter, pasture that is managed, suitable housing and sufficient supervision.

- Has a healthy diet.
  - » Sufficient food and clean water, and their body condition is kept within a normal range.

- Is able to behave normally.
  - » Adequate exercise provided, or the freedom to exercise, and appropriate training and handling.

- Has appropriate company.
  - » Sufficient socialisation opportunity and appropriate grouping for turnout or communal housing.

- Is protected from pain, suffering, injury and disease.
  - » Owners or keepers should be able to recognise the normal behaviour of their horse, recognise signs of ill health and provide routine health care (e.g. parasite control, vaccination, dental care, foot care).

Legal responsibilities

Duty of care

There are Codes of Practice for keeping horses, which support their welfare needs. Each part of the UK (i.e. Scotland, England, Wales, Northern Ireland) has its own welfare legislation and Code of Practice. Any person in charge of, or responsible for, a horse has a legal duty of care to protect their welfare. This includes having the appropriate knowledge and skills to care for the horse's needs, as well as knowing when and where to seek advice or help when necessary. If the horse's owner or carer is under 16 years old, their parent or guardian would be held responsible for the horse. The owner or keeper would maintain ultimate responsibility for their horse, even if they are away (e.g. on holiday), so they must leave their horse in the care of a suitably competent person who has the necessary authority to act in an emergency.

Passports and microchipping

Since 2004 it has been a legal requirement for all horses and ponies in the UK and the Republic of Ireland to have a passport that identifies the animal. This must be kept with the horse at all times, including when travelling. If the horse is sold, the passport must be handed over with the horse and the new owner's details added by the passport issuer.

All foals born after 1 July 2009 are required by law to be microchipped by the time their passport is applied for. Passport applications must be submitted within the same calendar year in which they were born, or within six months of their birth, whichever is the later.

Summary

- Assess signs of health — general body condition, coat condition, eyes, nose, appetite, droppings, movement, stance, normal behaviour.

- Get to know what is normal for your particular horse, so any changes can be noticed more quickly.

- Report any changes to a senior staff member, or your vet if you don't have anyone else to refer to.

- Assess body condition from all angles using key areas — crest, over the ribs and over the quarters.

- Ideal body condition — normal-shaped crest (no fat hump or hard fat); you should feel but not see the ribs; from behind you should see roughly rounded shape over the quarters with no channel running down the spine or concavity either side of the quarters; no bones protruding.

- Welfare needs of the horse — the horse should have a suitable environment to live in, a healthy diet, be able to behave normally, have appropriate company, and be protected from pain, suffering, injury and disease.

- Legal duty of care — applies to anyone (over 16 years of age) in charge of, or responsible for, a horse. Codes of Practice are produced supporting the Animal Welfare Act.

- Passports — legally all horses must have a passport, which should be kept with them.

- Microchipping — it is a legal requirement that all foals born after 1 July 2009 must be microchipped.

TRAINING TIPS

1. Assess a variety of horses with regard to their body condition and health.

2. If you get the opportunity, assist or observe at a veterinary visit.

3. Familiarise yourself with the legislation for animal welfare and the Code of Practice.

Chapter 6

Mucking Out

How to do a full muck out

Different types of bedding

Summary

Mucking Out

If it is not already, mucking out could soon become part of your daily routine. Clean stables are important to create a healthy environment for the horse. As with most things, the more mucking out you do, the quicker you become. And if you tackle things in a set order, it becomes automatic.

Many different types of bedding can be used and you may already have encountered various ways of managing them. The methods and bedding chosen depend on the needs of the horse and the preferences of the owner or yard manager, but it is useful to know the reasons for them.

When a horse is kept in, the stable must be mucked out and kept clean. Some yards will only have horses stabled overnight in winter; elsewhere they may be in nearly full-time. It often boils down to how much land is available for turnout.

If the horses are in nearly full-time, it is best to do a full muck out first thing, and skip out throughout the day. It is obviously easier to muck out an empty stable so, if you can, try to do it when the horse goes out into a turnout area or on a horse-walker. Another option is to find an empty stable or tie the horse up outside, making sure there are no tools or equipment nearby that the horse could injure himself on. If you need to leave the horse in the box, you will need to tie him up for safety and so you can move around him more easily.

What is skipping out?

Skipping out describes a quick stable tidy up, involving lifting out droppings and straightening up the bed.

If you have tied up the horse in the stable, a haynet should keep him occupied and out of your way while you muck out. Make sure you point your tools away from the horse; the fork, in particular, is quite dangerous if handled carelessly. It is usually best to do one side of the stable, then move the horse over to tackle the other side. Keep an eye on his facial expressions and what he's up to so you can react or intervene if necessary and keep you both safe.

How to do a full muck out

You will need a wheelbarrow, skip, shovel, broom and a fork. The type of fork depends on the type of bedding; a three- or four-pronged fork is best for straw and a shavings fork works with numerous beddings besides shavings, such as flax or wood pellets. If the horse is staying in the stable with you while you work, you will need to tie him up: you should leave the tools outside, as this gives you more room and is safer for the horse. Before you begin, remove any empty haynets and water buckets — this will stop the water buckets from getting dirty. The wheelbarrow can be positioned in the doorway: it is best to have the handles pointing out of the door away from the horse, so if the horse swings round he doesn't catch himself. If you leave some space at one side of the wheelbarrow you will be able to get out of the stable easily if you need to.

However, putting the wheelbarrow in the doorway can cause a hazard, so be careful and keep an eye on the horse. If the horse fidgets it may be best to close the door, and consider mucking out into a pile by the door or into a skip, to transfer to a wheelbarrow later. When working on a commercial yard you should always follow the yard's policy with regard to which method you use.

Removing dirty bedding

Start by lifting out all the droppings you can see. Many people do this by hand, wearing suitable rubber gloves. A fork can also be used. When you tip forkloads of droppings into the wheelbarrow, try to keep any clean bedding on the fork so it can be returned — it's expensive, so don't waste it. Next, sort through the rest of the bed; put wet, heavy bedding into the wheelbarrow, and clean bedding can be banked up the stable sides to air. As you remove wet or dirty bits, try to spread it out to the corners of the wheelbarrow and layer it up in order to minimise your visits to the muckheap. When you have removed all the dirty bedding, sweep the floor.

Banks are raised sections of bed next to the stable walls, and it's important to keep them clean. You could rotate the banks day by day, completely clearing under one of the three each day. Alternatively, you could pile bedding up three walls as you muck out, sweep the exposed floor, then pull the sides down into the middle of the stable and sweep the edges. Experiment to see what works best for you.

Mucking out a straw bed using a fork.

Clean bedding banked up two walls with the floor swept. This can be rotated each day so that each bank is cleaned regularly.

Putting the bed back down

After you have mucked out, pull the bedding down so it is even and flat. If the horse is staying in during the day you might put a thinner 'day bed' down, which is easier to keep clean, then put the rest down later on. There may be horses who need a thicker bed during the day too, if they have an injury and need support, for example. If the horse is turned out in the day you can put down the full bed straight away, or later on if the stable needs to air. To re-lay a full bed, fork the bedding from the banks to the centre of the stable and level it out. You need enough thickness to make the horse comfortable when lying down, with no scraping of elbows or hocks. As a guide, when you drop a straw fork straight into the bed, you should not hear its prongs hit the floor. If there is rubber matting underneath, the bed may be thinner, but must still be deep enough for warmth, comfort and to soak up urine. When it comes to topping up the bed, you can spread new bedding everywhere, or some people like to add it to the banks first and gradually work it into the main bed.

Shake out sections of straw as you add them to the bed, either by hand or with a fork.

Making banks

Some people use banks to make the bed warmer and smarter for the horse. Others use them to prevent the horse from becoming cast (see panel). If used for this latter reason they need to be very large and solid to make a 'fake wall'; this encourages the horse to roll further away from the actual wall, so he has more room to get up. Either make the banks before laying the middle of the bed, or by dragging bedding up into them with your fork afterwards. Fork them up and against the wall to shape them, then pat the central bed flat and push the banks securely against the walls. When the bed is finished, sweep any extra bedding tidily from the front of the stable to the bed. A clear space at the front of the stable looks neat and tidy and means water buckets stay relatively free from bedding.

Banks look nice and add some warmth to the horse when he lies down.

What do we mean by 'getting cast'?

A cast horse is one who has rolled in his stable and ended up with his legs against the wall without enough room to roll back again. Get help fast and be guided by someone with plenty of experience. Horses often panic when they get cast, so can injure themselves — or you — while thrashing around; it can be a very dangerous situation.

Water and hay

When you have finished mucking out, check that the horse has clean water and either hay or haylage (known as forage). The quantity will depend on the time of day (likely to be smaller amounts through the day and more at night). Water buckets should be scrubbed out with a brush, refilled and replaced. If the buckets have metal handles, they should be positioned towards the wall, away from the horse, so the horse doesn't get tangled up with them. If the stable has an automatic drinker, make sure it's clean. Water drinkers will need to be cleaned regularly, but you may need to turn the water off to do this.

The importance of mucking out

Clean stables are important if you want a healthy horse. Stables that aren't kept clean will begin to smell, particularly of ammonia from the horse's urine. Not only is this unpleasant for animals and owners alike (it's what catches in the back of the throat and makes your eyes sting in a dirty stable), it will also make the drinking water stale more quickly and could make horses reluctant to drink. The smell of ammonia may also attract flies in the summer. If a horse stands in dirty bedding for long periods it can contribute to the development of thrush (see Picking out feet) in his feet — which is easily prevented by a clean stable and picking out the feet twice daily.

Deep litter beds

Deep litter is a different bedding system that does not involve mucking out to the floor each day. All droppings are removed, but wet patches are levelled out, allowing a wet base to build up, with fresh bedding added on the top. Once the base has formed (which takes a couple of weeks), clean bedding is forked to the sides daily, the top of the wet patches is skimmed off to keep the base level, and clean bedding laid back down and topped up as necessary. The base can become quite deep, so you need to keep on top of it.

This is a useful labour-saving system and can save bedding costs. However, deep litter beds need to be completely emptied when they become too deep and this can be heavy, unpleasant work. These beds also need careful management so they do not become too dirty or wet, increasing the risk of thrush or infections in any cuts. Horses on deep litter beds will need their feet picked out more regularly to ensure they remain clean. Deep litter is not suitable for all horses, such as one who is restless, or who has developed the stereotypical behaviour known as 'box-walking'. They can also smell more than beds that are fully mucked out each day, because of the build-up of ammonia.

Keeping the stable clean throughout the day

The cleaner you can keep a stable the better; it will help make the bedding last longer and creates a nicer environment for the horse. Most yards will have a specific routine and stables will be skipped out at specific times, usually at midday then in the afternoon when the night beds are put down. If you go into the stable to groom or tack up, it is a good idea to skip it out too, to keep on top of the task and prevent both you and the horse from standing in droppings. Take in a skip (usually a big bucket or tub), and either fork droppings into it, or wear rubber gloves and use your hands. The skip will need to be emptied regularly into a wheelbarrow and the contents taken off to the muckheap.

Take the skip into the stable and lift the droppings into it.

Muckheaps

Some yards have a permanent muckheap area contained within three walls, perhaps with steps in it to help compact the muck and stack it up high. Or the yard may use a tractor to push back and squash down the muck. Other yards may have a heap that is not enclosed, requiring some care to tidy the edges. Another common option is a muck trailer that is taken away when full, but it will still take effort to keep it tidy and to fit a maximum load. All muckheaps need disposing of, which can be expensive; yards typically pay a contractor to remove the muck when the heap becomes too large.

Enclosed permanent muckheap that is pushed back by a tractor.

Muck trailers and containers can be easily removed to empty.

Different types of bedding

A range of beddings are available, with new types being developed all the time. Most importantly, the bedding chosen should suit the horse. Some have allergies and require one that is dust-free. Sometimes horses are inclined to eat certain bedding, like straw, which is a problem if you are trying to control their diet and, in some cases, can lead to colic.

Cost is usually an important factor, especially for commercial yards, with storage another important consideration. Some beddings are more compact than others and, if covered in strong plastic, it may be possible to store such bedding outside. A big factor is disposal; some bedding rots more easily than others and some makes for a larger muckheap than others.

Examples of some common types of bedding

Straw is popular and has been used as bedding for centuries. Straw beds can look smart, drain well and be warm and comfortable, although horses may be tempted to eat straw. It does not always absorb urine well, so works best with good drainage.

Wood shavings are also popular; they are absorbent and create an easily managed bed. Shavings can be produced as a by-product at sawmills, however these are often low quality and may contain splinters and other potential harmful waste. Therefore it is best to buy shavings produced specifically as horse bedding; some have had their dust extracted too.

Wood pellets are a form of compressed wood shavings. Water is added to make them expand, ready to be made into a bed. This type of bed is normally used like a deep litter system. Wood pellets come in plastic bags and take up less space than other bedding.

Shredded paper or cardboard can be bought in bales or collected as office waste. Shredded paper is highly absorbent, but can as a consequence be heavy to muck out and can blow about the yard, making it look untidy. Such bedding can be very cost-effective if collected as waste, provided that you look out for other hazards mixed in with the paper!

Bedding made from the chopped stems of flax and hemp plants are very absorbent options. The wet collects at the bottom of the bed, producing less odour in the stable as a result. These beddings often work best as semi-deep litter where a small base is left to build so the bed is more stable and does not slide around.

Rubber matting is often used as a base under any of the materials listed above. Although expensive to lay initially, less bedding is needed afterwards as the rubber reduces the risk of a horse lying on concrete and being injured. Rubber mats often come individually, which then fit together, but these should be lifted and the floor beneath cleaned several times a year. It is also possible to 'seal in' mats so no urine gets underneath, or opt for matting that comes in liquid form to produce a seamless finish and does not need lifting and cleaning. Mats should never be used without bedding and the bedding should be deep enough to allow the horse to lie down in comfort.

Advantages and disadvantages of different bedding

Bedding type	Cost	Dust-free?	Horse likely to eat?	Rotting time	Absorbency
Straw	Low	No	Yes	Fastest	Low
Shavings	Medium	Depends on product	No	Slowest	High
Paper and cardboard	Medium	Yes	No	Medium	Medium
Wood pellets	Medium	Yes	No	Medium	High
Hemp	High	Yes	No	Medium	High
Flax	Medium	Yes	No	Medium	High

Summary

- Stables should be kept clean to maintain a healthy environment for the horse.

- When mucking out, all droppings and wet areas are removed.

- When skipping out, the droppings are removed and the bed is tidied.

- The bed should be thick enough so that when the horse lies down, he does not scrape his legs. As a guide, if you drop the fork straight down you should not hear the prongs hit the floor.

- Bedding can be banked around the walls to prevent draughts and can also prevent the horse from becoming cast.

- Water drinkers and buckets should be cleaned after mucking out to prevent the water from becoming stale.

TRAINING TIPS

1. Have a look at different types of bedding used on different yards.

2. Speak to horse owners about the types of bedding they use, and why.

3. Time how long it takes you to muck out and try to better your time without losing the quality of your work until you are efficient (15 minutes is average for a yard worker).

Chapter 7

Feeding Horses

Feeding Horses

Feeding horses should essentially be really easy ... feed too little and they will be thin; feed too much and they will become fat. In practice, it is not quite that simple, with many other factors to consider to keep horses happy and healthy. There is a copious amount of information available about feeds and feeding, and hundreds of feeds and supplements available, as a visit to any feed merchant testifies. Each of them is marketed in a way that makes them appear indispensable. So how should you decide what to feed? By remembering some basic concepts it can be almost as easy as 'feed more if they are thin, feed less if they are fat'.

What do horses need?

It's useful to start by understanding what a horse needs to survive, and how horses evolved before we got our hands on them. In the wild they would not have access to cereals and grains (barley and oats, etc.) but would spend up to 70 per cent of their time consuming grass, plants and pickings from hedges and trees.

Importantly, the grass they ate was of quite low nutritional value, so large volumes would have been consumed to produce the energy (calories) needed.

Most horse pasture today has been improved by farming at some point, so is often richer in sugar and energy than many horses and ponies need, resulting in excess weight and perhaps metabolic disorders and behavioural problems. To maintain a normal body weight, they need to eat around 2 per cent of their body weight in fibre (based on the horse being the correct weight and eating average quality fibre). Some put on weight easily (e.g. native breeds) or are already too fat and should be given less than this, but no horse or pony should have less than 1.5 per cent of their body weight per day as fibre (unless under veterinary supervision). Their digestive system works best by having a steady trickle of fibre passing through it; feeding less than this quantity of fibre can cause illness and gut problems such as ulcers and colic.

Look at the table overleaf showing how much fibre different horses and ponies need per day. Equines doing no work normally live entirely on fibre, as do many in light work.

> **What do we mean by fibre?**
>
> *Lots of foods are composed of fibre, be that long fibre such as grass, hay or haylage, or short or chopped fibre, which includes chaffs (straw, hay, alfalfa). Other fibre sources are bagged feeds such as fibre cubes, alfalfa pellets and sugar beet.*

**Approximate weight of different horses and ponies feed needed per day
if eating 2 per cent of their body weight**

Type of horse	Approximate body weight	Feed needed (2 per cent of body weight)
13.2hh Native pony	350kg (770lb)	7kg (15.4lb)
14.2hh Native x Thoroughbred	400kg (880lb)	8kg (17.6lb)
15hh Polo pony	450kg (990lb)	9kg (19.8lb)
15hh Cob	500 kg (1,100lb)	10kg (22.0lb)
16hh Thoroughbred	550kg (1,210lb)	11kg (24.2lb)
16.2hh Sports horse	600kg (1,320lb)	12kg (26.4lb)
17hh Hunter	700kg (1,540lb)	14kg (30.8lb)

Feedstuffs

The healthiest feed regime is a high-fibre diet with added cereal/grain kept to the minimum practical. The main part of the diet should be grass, hay or haylage.

Hay

Hay is dried grass that is cut in the summer and left to dry out in the sun, getting turned over a couple of times by farm machinery. Lots of different grasses appear in hay and this affects the amount of energy or calories it will give the horse. Don't assume that any hay suits any horse or pony; the only way to know its nutritional value is through laboratory analysis. The hay's maker or buyer should advise you on its energy value so you can work out if you need to feed more or less of it. In general, hay is either meadow hay cut from old pasture that has produced only grass for a long time (including lots of different grasses and herbs), or seed hay that has been sown specifically for the purpose and normally contains only a couple of grasses.

Haylage

Haylage is also dried grass, cut like hay, but baled while still a little damp. It is then wrapped in plastic so it is airtight, and bacteria within the bale ferment the sugars in the grass. The quality can vary much more than hay and it is important to check each bale as you open it in case it has 'spoiled'. If there are any holes in the wrap, or a lot of soil has been pulled in with the grass, it can go 'off' and will be unsafe to feed. The wetness of the haylage will vary too. Drier is normally best for horses, as wetter haylage can cause some to develop diarrhoea. As with hay, the grasses and energy content can vary between batches. Having a higher water content than hay, it is also heavier, so you might have to feed more to give the same amount of energy as hay (think about pasta; 100g (3.5oz) dry pasta might weigh 200g (7oz) once cooked, but will still have the same energy). There are many different varieties of haylage, all with different energy levels that will be indicated on the packaging. This information will help you decide the best type for the horse, and the appropriate quantity.

Bagged feed

Most yards have a variety of feeds in the feed room. The ones used for horses at rest or in low-level work are likely to be the following.

Different types of bagged feeds	
 *Basic chaff*  *Alfalfa*	**Chaff/chopped fibre** Often used to bulk out bucket food so it is not eaten too fast (fibre takes longer to chew than grains), which can cause some horses to choke or get colic. These foods are often made from chopped grass, hay, straw or alfalfa and sometimes mixed with oil or molasses. The feed sacks tell you which ones have higher energy levels. Sometimes chaff is used as a disguise to hide the taste of a supplement or medication. Some chopped fibre-based feeds contain added vitamins and minerals and so can be fed as a complete bucket feed.

Different types of bagged feeds

Horse/pony cubes

Mix

Coarse mix or cubes

These are essentially similar products, but in the latter the ingredients are pressed together into pellets. Cubes often cost a bit less than the equivalent mix. A huge range of mixes/cubes are sold under different categories based on the ingredients included. Ones classed as 'cool', 'leisure' or 'high-fibre' are normally high in fibre and low in cereals, and thus ideal for horses in light work who need a little bit more than just grass and hay. (Remember, there is nothing wrong with feeding a horse only fibre-based feed if his calorie needs are met.) A mix or cube that is high energy (usually for competition or racehorses) will typically have lots of cereal grains and less fibre. If you open a bin full of mix in the feed room, you may be able to tell from the ratio of cereals whether it is a higher- or lower-energy feed. The problem with cubes or pellets is they all look the same! Only the bag can tell you what is in them.

Dry sugar beet pellets

Dry sugar beet shreds

Dry sugar beet flakes

Soaked sugar beet ready to feed

Sugar beet

Sugar beet is a really good and relatively cheap fibre feed. It is a by-product from the sugar refining industry, though its name is a bit misleading as actually there is not much sugar left in the product we feed horses. Sugar beet comes as a dry feed either in cubes, shreds or flakes. It MUST be soaked before being fed (see 'preparing feed').

Different types of bagged feeds	
 *Balancer*	**Balancers** If feeding a horse or pony only grass or hay there may be some missing vitamins and minerals, and balancers are an ideal way to top those up. Similarly, if you feed less than the full recommended amount of a bagged feed, the recipient may not get enough vitamins and minerals. Balancers solve this while supplying minimal additional calories. They normally come as small pellets, which you feed in fairly small amounts, often using a specific measuring cup.

Rules of feeding

The 'rules of feeding' for horses and ponies have been around for a very long time, and understanding them will go a long way to helping you feed well.

1. Provide fresh, clean water at all times

Every tiny cell in the body needs water to work. Similar to us, drinking inadequate amounts results in horses being unable to work or perform well. In more extreme situations, dehydration can result in serious illness and disease. An average 16hh horse will drink between 30 and 70 litres (53 and 123 pints) of water a day (approx. two to five standard plastic buckets). Water must be clean and checked regularly, as 'tainted' water will deter a horse from drinking; would you drink a glass of water that had been sitting in a dusty room for a couple of days? If the yard has automatic drinkers it is important to observe that they're actually being used, as it is difficult to tell how much has been drunk.

2. Always weigh feeds

A full scoop of one feed may weigh much less than the same volume of another. Similarly, it is hard to judge comparable weights of hay and haylage consistently by eye, so a balance to weigh nets or bags is a good idea. Weigh a scoopful of bagged feed at the outset to work out how many scoops a horse needs (taking care to keep using the same-sized scoop afterwards).

Weighing hay using a spring balance.

3. Feed little and often

Horses' digestive tracts have evolved to work best when small amounts of fibre are almost constantly passing through. You may have heard the term 'horses are trickle feeders'. The horse has a relatively small stomach (a 16hh horse has a stomach about the size of a rugby ball) and it works best when it is about two-thirds full. If you feed more than this in one go, the stomach is not going to work properly. At best, it will be wasteful, with some food passing straight through the horse before it has broken down and been digested properly. At worst, it may trigger colic. At the other end of the scale, if you leave horses for long periods without food, the gut does not work properly and both the stomach and intestine can develop painful ulcers.

4. Feed plenty of forage

The best feed regime for a healthy gut is 100 per cent forage or fibre. This requires horses to spend more time chewing, the food trickles through the digestive system more regularly and the gut is rarely empty. It is the feed horses evolved on — although a balancer or supplement to ensure a balanced diet may be advisable.

5. Feed good-quality feeds (forage and bagged feed)

Low-quality feed may not contain enough calories, vitamins and minerals to keep the horse healthy. More importantly, a dusty or mouldy feed may damage breathing and produce toxins, which can cause illness, colic and generally upset the digestive system.

6. Make changes to feed and forage gradually

The horse's large intestine is home to billions of 'friendly' bacteria that help digest food. They change in response to different types of food (like fibre vs. cereals) so if you suddenly change feed (even switching to a different batch of hay or grass), the bacteria don't get time to adjust. Some of what you feed will not be digested properly, or the change may trigger colic. It is best to swap feeds over a period of a couple of weeks, gradually reducing the proportion of old feed while increasing the new one. When changing fields, especially turning out after the winter, start with short periods in the new field and increase gradually over a week or so.

7. Do not work hard straight after a large bucket feed

It takes time for a big meal (especially one containing cereals) to empty from the stomach, and when the horse begins exercise, blood is diverted from the digestive tract to power breathing and muscles. This means that the food will sit undigested and may be uncomfortable for the horse, rather like us going for a run straight after a big meal. If feeding forage or a small fibre-based feed in a bucket, there's no need to wait before exercising. In fact, this can help horses who are prone to stomach ulcers as a layer of fibre protects the stomach from being irritated by acids.

8. Keep to a routine

Horses thrive on a good routine and your aim should be to keep them as happy and relaxed as possible. One of the biggest contributors to colic and gastric ulcers is stress; horses fed at regular times stay happier.

9. Feed according to body weight, work done and temperament

As explained earlier, a horse who is the correct weight needs to eat two per cent of his total body weight in fibre for maintenance, but every horse and pony needs slightly different things. The first thing to consider is their body weight: are they too fat, too thin or just right? Horses in work need more calories of course, but it is really important to feed them to replace energy they have used, rather than feed them up beforehand (which would lead to them becoming fat or could cause colic). You should also feed less on days off, from the evening before until the evening after. Temperament is important too; horses can respond to various energy sources differently.

Feed quality

Comparison of good-quality (left) and bad-quality (right) hay.

Comparison of good-quality (left) and bad-quality (right) haylage.

Mouldy feed.

How to recognise good and bad feed

Type of feed	Good	Bad
Hay	• Golden/slightly green • Dry • Sweet smell • No mould • Cool to touch • No dust when shaken • Not too many seeds and short fragments • No weeds or ragwort (see Bad)	• Brown/grey • Damp • Smells musty • Mouldy • Warm/hot • Dusty when shaken • Soil mixed in • Weeds, ragwort (NEVER FEED) • Dirt on one end of bale from sitting on ground
Haylage	• Golden slightly green • Damp/slightly wet • Sweet smell • No mould (naturally occurring yeasts are fine, often seen as small white lumps) • Cool to touch • No holes in wrap • Bale same quality throughout	• Brown, sludgy colour • Very wet, like silage • Alcoholic smell • Mould (green, red particularly bad) • Warm or hot • Holes in wrap • Patch on bale that is very wet/ mouldy (toxins can be in the rest of the bale too!)
Bagged feed	• Fresh, sweet smell • Well-formed components • Glossy look • No damage to bag	• Smells musty • Components broken down • Dull colours • Dusty coating • Clumps of feed stuck together (fine for molassed feeds!) • Mould • Hole in bag • Evidence of rodents (chewed bag/droppings)

Feed room hygiene

To maintain feed quality it is important to keep the feed room clean and tidy. Feed should be kept in rodent-proof bins, spillages should be cleaned up as soon as possible and the floor around and behind feed bins swept out regularly, to deter pests. Many yards have a cat or two; these are brilliant for helping to discourage mice and rats. All feed buckets, scoops and stirrers should be washed daily to keep them clean and fresh. There is no point putting good-quality feed into a dirty bucket or contaminating a good bag of feed with a mouldy scoop. This also prevents cross-contamination with medications or supplements.

Preparing feed

Feed preparation typically includes soaking or steaming forage or sugar beet. You will need to concentrate; it could be dangerous for the wrong horse to receive non-prescribed medication. Horses competing at high levels may be drug-tested, so the wrong feed or even sharing a stirrer can cause a problem. Once feeds are made up, they should be kept covered so you don't inadvertently poison your dog or help feed rats.

Keep feeds covered.

Keep buckets and scoop clean.

It is a good idea to dampen feeds with water to make them easier to consume. Horses who are known to choke will normally have very wet, 'soupy' feed. Follow any such instructions carefully; dealing with a sloppy feed is much better than calling the vet. Some carrots may help tempt a fussy eater, but be sure to cut them lengthways so they don't get stuck in the throat.

Soaking sugar beet

As mentioned earlier, sugar beet MUST be soaked before feeding, as it will swell to around three times its volume when it comes into contact with water. Colic or a ruptured stomach can result if large amounts of dry sugar beet are fed by mistake.

As a rough guide, pellets need to be soaked for at least 24 hours and shreds for 12 hours before feeding. Flakes sold as 'quick soak' are normally pre-treated so they can be ready in as little as 15 minutes. Pellets are usually cheaper, but flakes can be useful in the summer when the heat can make soaked beet go off fast. It is crucial to read the manufacturer's instructions to see how long and how much water is needed for each brand. A label on the sugar beet bin/soaking bucket is useful, on which to write the day and time it was put in to soak.

Soaking and steaming forage

Horses with breathing problems often need soaked or steamed hay. Hay should be fully immersed in water for 10 minutes (not just sprinkled with a hose), to remove airborne dust. The downside is that even a short soak washes away some of the nutrients too (although this is sometimes useful — see next paragraph). Soaking also increases the bacteria content in the hay, thus reducing its hygienic quality. Steaming with a purpose-built machine is the best way to improve hay for horses with breathing problems, as the high temperature kills bacteria without losing nutrients. These processes are not a way to make bad hay okay, however — owners and yard managers should always buy the best quality they can.

Some overweight equines, or those with metabolic problems, may need to have their hay soaked to wash out some of the sugars and nutrients. This requires a longer soaking; your yard manager should be able to advise.

Once you have soaked your hay you should feed it within a few hours before it dries out and bacteria start building back up again.

Hay needs to be fully immersed in water; this hay is being pushed down.

Different ways to feed hay and haylage

There are lots of different ways to feed hay to stabled horses, and which you use often comes down to time, cost and the yard owner's preference (see table below). If feeding hay in the field, some people put large bales out, while others prefer small amounts every day. In this case, consider where you put it so horses do not fight over it; some guard their food fiercely! During wet periods, it may also be helpful to change the placement of large bales, to prevent the same piece of ground getting very poached.

If you are putting out loose hay in the field, try to make lots of small piles (ideally a couple more than there are horses in the field), and space them three to four horses' lengths apart, well away from the fence line, so the horses can find their own piles and relax to eat.

Different methods of feeding hay and haylage in a stable

Method	Cost (approx.)	Reduced waste?	Safe for horse?	Impact on horse
Loose on floor	Free!	Horse can drag into bed and soil it	Very	Natural feeding position, good for breathing
Haynet	£5–£15 each but need to be replaced from time to time	Little waste	If tied up correctly, but can come down and get tangled in horse's legs	Pulling out of a haynet can sometimes build up muscles on the neck in the wrong place for riding
Hayrack	£30–£50	Little waste	Very, if safely positioned	Same as haynet and can get seeds/dust in eyes
Haybar/floor rack	£50–£80	But less likely to be dragged into bed than if on floor	Yes, but horse could lift a foreleg into it (construction should mean low injury chance)	Natural feeding position, good for breathing

Using haynets

There is a bit of an art to filling haynets, as you will know if you've ever struggled with one. Looping one of the top holes on a hook will help, as will asking someone else to hold one side, or gripping a side between your knees. If you don't need it right away, tying the drawstring in a quick-release knot should stop it opening and spilling out again in the meanwhile. When you tie it in the stable, keep the net as high as you can so that, as the horse empties it, the bottom never ends up low enough for him to catch a leg in it. Use a quick-release knot to tie it up.

i. *Thread the drawstring through the ring and pull the net right up to the ring at the start so, as you tie it up, it does not slide back down too much.*

ii. *Put the drawstring back through a hole near the bottom of the net.*

iii. *Pull the drawstring up tight; this will help to keep the haynet high enough when tied up.*

iv. *Tie a quick-release knot.*

v. *Turn the net round so the knot is against the wall so there is less chance of the horse undoing it!*

Summary

- Remember to follow the rules of feeding:
  1. Provide fresh, clean water at all times.
  2. Always weigh feeds.
  3. Feed little and often.
  4. Feed plenty of forage.
  5. Feed good-quality feeds (forage and bagged feed).
  6. Make changes to feed and forage gradually.
  7. Do not work hard straight after a large bucket feed.
  8. Keep to a routine.
  9. Feed according to body weight, work done and temperament.

- Commonly used feeds are hay, haylage, chaff, mixes, cubes, balancers and sugar beet.

- Always use high-quality feed. Keep feed in good condition by storing it correctly and following good hygiene practices.

- Horses and ponies need to eat around two per cent of their body weight in forage per day. They should never get less than 1.5 per cent to protect gut health.

- Prepare feed as per instructions; feeds are devised for individual horses based on lots of different variables. Not sticking to this can result in weight gain/loss or even conditions such as colic.

TRAINING TIPS

1. Explore the feed room and see if you can identify what is there without reading feed bag labels first.

2. Next time you visit a feed merchant, have a look at the variety of things on offer.

3. Every time you go to a new yard, take the time to look at their hay and haylage to examine its quality.

4. Weigh a level scoop full of chaff, dry sugar beet, mix and cubes. Note the differences.

Chapter 8

Grooming Horses

Grooming Horses

Grooming is one of the most important skills you will learn when caring for horses. Aside from making a horse look clean and smart, there are other more important benefits. It's an excellent time for you and your horse to get to know one another as you observe how horses respond and react to things. You will also learn where they do and don't like to be touched, and have the chance to work out how best you can communicate with them. Once you know how a horse responds and acts normally this gives you a great reference point to compare against when you are worried that something might be wrong.

While grooming, you should check the horse's whole body for lumps, bumps, heat, scabs, swelling and any unusual sensitivity. Anything out of the ordinary may be an early warning that something is wrong. Grooming has further health benefits for the horse, such as keeping the skin in good condition (in the same way that brushing and washing your hair helps your scalp), and improving circulation and muscle tone through the pressure and release of brushes against the large muscle areas (in a similar way to massage).

Grooming lets you build a relationship with a horse.

Equipment

There are many items of grooming kit available, some of which are mentioned here. Most of them are variations on common items. Before using any piece of your grooming kit, take a minute to think about which part of the body you are about to use it for. Consider the job you need it to do. Is it to remove dried mud, get rid of hair when the horse is moulting, or simply flick off light dust? Is it too hard for sensitive areas, especially if the horse is clipped? You may need to use softer brushes if this is the case.

Like people, some horses are more ticklish than others (e.g. a Thoroughbred will typically be more sensitive than a native pony) and some have certain areas where they are particularly ticklish. Once you know a horse you can customise what you do with that individual; and he will appreciate you taking the trouble to consider his needs.

Items of a grooming kit

Plastic curry comb
— short, stiff bristles to remove mud and loose hair and to clean brushes.

Rubber curry comb
— short rubber teeth or pimples to dislodge grease loose hair and mud.

Mane comb
— metal or plastic comb with long teeth for combing out the mane.

Metal curry comb
— sharp metal teeth to clean brushes, not for use on the horse.

Water brush
— medium stiffness bristles for bathing the horse and laying the mane or cleaning stains in the coat.

Dandy brush
— stiff bristles to remove mud and dirt.

Flick brush
— long bristles to remove dust and grease.

Body brush
— soft bristles to remove dust and grease.

A number of different sponges for cleaning the eyes/nose/dock and bathing the horse.

Stable rubber
— cloth or towel to wipe off dust and grease and help to make the coat shine.

Hoofpick
— to remove mud, stones and dirt from the horse's feet.

Sweat scraper
— plastic with a rubber edge to remove water after bathing or washing off.

Mane and tail brush — similar to human hairbrush for brushing/detangling the mane and tail.

Caring for grooming equipment

Logically, it's easier to get a horse clean if your implements are clean first. It is important to wash brushes regularly in an antibacterial soap, both to remove any bacteria that may build up and to help the kit last longer. It is important to have a separate grooming kit for each horse to help prevent the spread of any infection.

General tips for grooming

It is best to tie up your horse before grooming, as a ticklish horse may be reluctant to stand still. Depending on the weather and facilities available, it can be a good idea to take the horse out of the stable to avoid any dust or dirt settling back on to his coat and to prevent you and the horse from breathing it in. However, this is not always possible and some horses are more relaxed in their stable. If you are grooming indoors, take the water bucket out beforehand to prevent a film of dust from settling on it. A haynet can often help occupy the horse and keep him more relaxed. Wherever you decide to tie up, try to avoid being too close to any walls or hazards, like wheelbarrows and yard equipment, so that you won't get trapped or squashed if the horse swings round. Before you start, place everything within easy reach for you but out of reach of the horse so he can't stand on it. It is important that the horse knows where you are, so keep talking, and remember that a horse can't see you immediately in front or behind him.

When grooming the body, aim to work in a systematic way by working from the head to the tail, then repeating this on the opposite side. This also allows you to brush in the same direction as the hair. Some horses may be a little sensitive when you reach certain areas, e.g. the stomach or stifle, so keep an eye on their expressions and reactions — ears flicked back may mean they are uncomfortable. Too light a pressure when brushing may tickle a sensitive horse more than a longer, firmer stroke.

Practice will help you develop good technique and, again, a horse's reactions will guide you. Keep your body close enough to the horse to be effective but take care about where you stand. You may need to move out of the way quickly, so bending your knees rather than kneeling when working low down on the legs or stomach is safer. If you keep your free hand gently in contact with the horse as you work you can quickly feel if he tenses up and so react appropriately.

Choose a brush appropriate to your task. You wouldn't brush your hair with a large, stiff yard brush; in the same way, choose something kinder and softer (e.g. a body brush) to groom sensitive areas such as the horse's face. The wrong choice can upset even the most docile animal. Aim to be effective without making the horse uncomfortable. To remove dried mud from the horse's legs it is better to use a brush with stiffer bristles (e.g. dandy brush), so long as the horse does not overreact to this.

Some horses can be anxious when their heads are groomed (often because of a previous bad experience), so it is best to untie the quick-release knot, leaving the rope loosely through the string of the tie-ring, while you are doing this, in case the horse pulls back. Remember to re-tie the rope afterwards. Don't startle the horse by moving your hand and brush too quickly towards his head, and be very careful around the eyes. Some horses relax better if you face the same way as them while you brush the head, slipping your free arm under the chin and resting your hand gently on the front of the face. This can also keep the head steady. Make sure you do not put your head in front of the horse, as it may be hit if the horse moves his head suddenly.

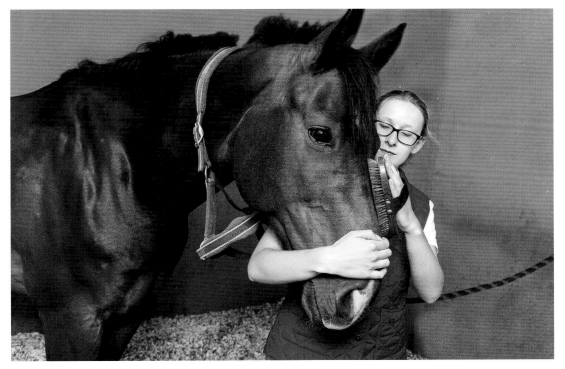

Gently holding the head can make it easier to brush.

Depending on the weather and time of year, you may want to groom without completely removing the horse's rug. If it is even slightly breezy, this may be better done indoors so that the rug does not blow off. Fold the front back so that it only covers from behind where the saddle would sit, and groom the uncovered area. Then fold the rug forwards to cover the shoulder and saddle area and repeat. This is known as 'quartering'.

When folding the rug over, unfasten all the buckles and straps first so that it will not get caught round the legs or neck if it accidentally slips off. The surcingles need to be tied up by knotting them together, and leg straps (if you have them) need to be fastened back up on the outside of the leg, so that they don't dangle or get caught on anything. Fold the rug too far back and it is likely to slide off the back and on to the floor; too far the other way and it

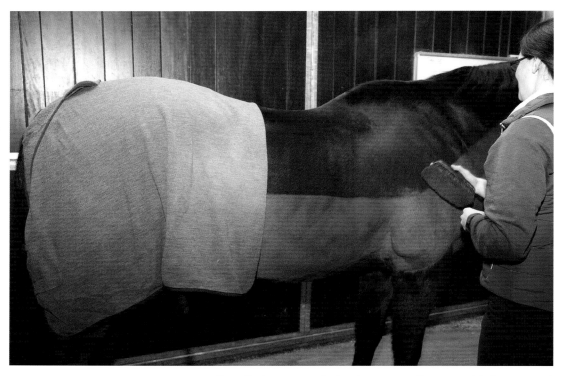

Keep the horse warm by leaving a rug on the area not being groomed.

may slide down the neck and over the head if the horse puts his head down. Once you have finished grooming, replace and refasten the rug.

The thorough groom

Ideally, to encourage a healthy skin and coat, a horse should be given a thorough groom every day. However, people lead busy lives and sometimes a quick groom can save time. If you are caring for a horse or pony who lives out and is not rugged you need to avoid over-grooming as you will remove natural oils that are necessary for keeping the rain off the skin. In this situation, it is particularly important to pay attention to the feet and make sure you look at and feel all areas of the body every day to check for cuts and scrapes. It is important to pay particular attention to any soreness caused by muddy wet conditions on the legs, as this can lead to mud fever.

Picking out feet

The old saying 'No foot, no horse' is very true, and picking out the hooves is one of the most important elements of grooming. It's your chance to look out for a loose shoe, a puncture wound or any other issue that may cause potential lameness. Balancing half a tonne on four small hooves is a feat in itself, so we need to keep the feet clean and well trimmed/shod to keep them healthy. A stone or pebble wedged in a hoof can be enough to cause pain or lameness, so good hoof hygiene is essential.

Make sure the horse is aware of what you are doing. Run your closest hand down his body and then down the leg before trying to lift the foot. Don't just lunge suddenly at the foot; your reward may be a startled jump, or even a kick. Most horses happily pick their foot up as a hand is run down their leg with the simple command 'Up'. Sometimes they may need a little encouragement by squeezing gently just above the fetlock joint. Once up, it is best to hold the foot by the hoof using the hand closest to the horse. Holding the leg any higher may make the foot flop around, making the job harder. To minimise the risk of a knock if the horse unexpectedly pulls his leg back, hold a forefoot with your arm across the back of the leg and round the inside of the foot. A hind foot is best held with the arm across the front of the leg and round the inside of the foot. This way, the horse's leg will move away from you, not towards you, if the foot is suddenly put down.

Always hold the forefoot with your arm at the back of the leg. When picking out the foot, use a heel-to-toe direction into a skip.

Always hold the hind foot with your arm at the front of the leg.

Hold the foot firmly, with the hoofpick in your free hand. Moving the hoofpick from heel to toe, scrape any dirt and debris out of the hoof, taking care around the sensitive frog. Keep the point of the hoofpick facing away from your body so that, if your hand slips, the sharp part of the hoofpick moves away from you. It is important to remove the dirt thoroughly from all areas of the foot to avoid an unpleasant bacterial infection called thrush. Pay attention to the deep channels either side of the frog and at the heels under the ends of the shoe where it is easy for fragments to become trapped. Some hoofpicks have a little brush on the opposite side from the hook, and this can be handy for dislodging any last little pieces of grime. You might need a separate stiff-bristled brush if the hoofpick does not have one.

> ### What is the frog?
>
> *The frog is a triangular structure on the bottom of the horse's foot. Most of the hoof is made of hard horn, rather like our fingernails, that have no sensation. The frog is made of softer tissue rather like a pad on a dog's foot and is sensitive, so if you are too rough with a hoofpick it may cause pain.*

It is a good idea to pick the feet out into a skip or flat bucket, especially in the stable, to avoid dirt and stones going into the bedding or even straight back into the horse's feet. If grooming outside, this saves you from having to sweep the yard afterwards. Most horses get used to the skip if it is introduced to them carefully but, if not, pick out on to the floor and clean up any dirt afterwards. Avoid moving the skip suddenly, which may startle the horse. If you are not sure how a particular horse might react to one, ask a more experienced colleague first.

Removing mud, dirt and grease

Before you can make the horse really clean and shiny, you need to remove the worst of the grime such as mud, sweat and stable stains. A dandy brush or a plastic curry comb can be very useful for removing mud and dirt, particularly on longer-haired horses. Next, you need to lift any grease and dust from the surface of the coat. There are a few different options for this, and which to use will depend on both personal preference (which will come from experience) and the individual horse. The rubber curry comb is great for this job. The horse will often enjoy the circular scrubbing motion you should use with it, particularly if he is itchy, and many will try to groom you back, or their top lip may twitch!

With the dust and grease now on the coat surface, you can brush it away. A flick brush with long, stiff bristles can be great for this, although be careful to do this downwind if you don't want the dust to settle back on the horse, or even get in your eyes. A body brush can also be used for this job, again in a 'flicking' motion. Remove dust from the brushes regularly as you groom by scraping them against a metal curry comb. Holding the metal curry comb in your spare hand enables you to do this as you go, ideally every few strokes (turn it so the teeth are pointed away from you and the horse when not in use). Try to move your arms away from the horse and towards the floor slightly as you do this, to steer the dust away from your clean horse.

Using the rubber curry comb in small circles is great for lifting the grease to the surface.

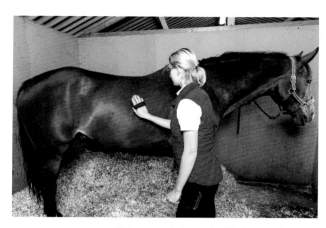

Using a body brush to lift dust and grease.

A clean brush makes it easier to groom the horse.

The mane and tail

Once the basic dirt has been removed, brush the mane and tail before polishing the body, so that any loose hair and dirt in these areas is dispersed first. The aim is to remove any dirt and tangles without pulling the hair out. There are various options for this, e.g. mane comb, body brush, mane and tail brush, and some are more effective than others. The gentlest method is separating the hairs with your fingers, although this is very time-consuming, especially with bushy-tailed horses. Sparing use of a mane and tail conditioning product can help to brush tangles out of a tail. This will make the hairs slip past each other; fewer hairs are pulled out and the job can be quicker. Just a word of warning — avoid using this on the mane of a ridden horse as it can make everything slippery, reins included.

Stand slightly to the side as you brush the tail so that the horse can see you. For logical reasons, it is sensible to avoid being directly behind the hind legs. Using one hand to hold the bulk of the tail and the other to brush, brush a very small section of hair at a time and add a few more hairs progressively until you have worked your way through the whole tail. It may help to hold the tail a little way from the bottom if it is particularly tangled and brush out the very end first as this is generally where the worst knots are.

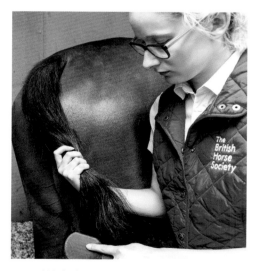

Work through the tail from a safe position.

To brush or comb out the mane, it is easiest to start at the top, behind the ears, and work down, a section at a time and brushing from the root to the tip. This helps it to lie neatly on one side

95

of the neck and removes any mud hidden after a good roll in the field. The forelock is best brushed at the same time as the rest of the head when the horse is untied.

Creating a shine and final touches

After you have removed the worst of the dirt and grease, and combed out the mane and tail, it's time to put some serious effort in with a body brush. By using reasonable pressure with nice long brush strokes you will lift the last bits of dust and smooth and polish the coat. Use the body brush and metal curry comb together as described earlier to keep the brush clean. Once you have been over the whole horse, a quick wipe over with a soft cloth adds a final gleam and removes any last traces of dirt. An old cloth or spare tea towel is ideal for this.

A method called 'hot clothing' can also be used, where you very lightly dampen the cloth in hot water before running it over the horse. The heat and moisture attracts dust from the horse to the cloth. This can be preferable to using a brush, which will flick dust into the air rather than holding on to it. Hot clothing is really handy in the winter when it is too cold to remove stubborn grease by bathing a horse.

Pay special attention to the eyes, nose and underneath the dock to avoid irritation or infection. Use a separate sponge for each, preferably of different colours so that you don't get them muddled up and cause cross-contamination. If you suspect any infection then use a small ball of dampened cotton wool and throw it away immediately after use. When cleaning the eyes and nose remember to untie the quick-release knot in case the horse pulls back. You should never attempt to clean the eyeball; concentrate instead on the area around it, removing any crusty dirt in the corners. Wipe away from the eye on to the surrounding area so there is no danger of wiping dirt into the eye. The horse may find it a bit tickly having his nose wiped, so use fairly firm strokes from the inside to outside of the nostril. You should aim to clean only the visible area; don't insert the sponge any higher.

To clean underneath the dock, pay attention to any dried bits of manure. You may need plenty of warm water to loosen it. Work from top to bottom so that any dirty water drips away from the clean parts. Some horses are not keen on being touched in this area and may clamp their tail down or warn you off by lifting a hind leg. Approach the task gently and quietly for best effect.

Be gentle when using a sponge to clean underneath the dock area and position yourself safely.

Other aspects of cleaning horses

The quick groom

There is no harm in a quick groom occasionally if you're short of time, although the feet should always be picked out and feet/shoes checked. It is a good idea to remove mud from the legs so that you can check thoroughly for signs of injury. You then need to clear dirt or mud from areas where tack or rugs will sit as this can cause rubbing and soreness, and to check for any problems.

Brushing/washing-off after work

After riding and untacking, the horse needs a brush or wash off to make him comfortable. If the horse is not sweaty, a quick brush off may suffice, paying particular attention to the girth and saddle areas, around the ears and under where any boots have been, to prevent grease from building up. As you run your hands over the horse, check again for any injury or rubs — it's post exercise that you're likely to spot any signs that the tack may be rubbing. Likewise a horse may have struck one leg with another or scraped himself against an arena wall or board. It is good practice to get into the habit of having a good check over after untacking.

If the weather is warm and the horse is sweaty, it can be a good idea to wash him off and then allow him to dry in the sun/warm air. To avoid chilling the horse in colder weather, it may be better to brush sweat off after he's dried.

A simple bucket and sponge works well for a wash-off, but you will need to keep changing the water as it gets dirty. Alternatively, you could use a hosepipe that allows a steady stream of clean water, but not all horses enjoy this and you will still need to use a bucket and sponge for sensitive areas such as the head and ears. Again, try to have someone holding the horse for you, or at least untie him as you wash sensitive places including the head. Some yards have a designated wash-off area, some even with warm water but, if not, you need to find a suitable place near a drain. Use a sweat scraper after washing-off to remove any excess water and to help the horse dry more quickly. Use it in a sweeping motion in the same direction as you would groom. If it is cold you will need to put a cooler rug on afterwards to stop the horse getting a chill.

Pay attention to any sweaty areas.

Bathing

Sometimes — e.g. before a show or when the horse has become really greasy — you may want to give the horse an all-over wash. Do not be tempted to use this instead of grooming, though, as you will lose the wider benefits described earlier.

As with grooming, place all the equipment you need nearby, but not where you may trip over it. You can use a water brush on areas such as the legs, or elsewhere if the horse is rather hairy and the sponge is not so effective. Some types of rubber curry comb can also be useful, and give the horse a bit of a massage at the same time. As with your own hair, wet the coat thoroughly before applying shampoo, work it into the hair and massage the roots next to the skin. Wash right down to the skin of the mane and tail so that any scurf is washed out, scrubbing with your fingertips if necessary. To rinse off and dry, follow the procedure described above for washing-off.

It may be easier to wash the head without the headcollar in the way. You may fasten it instead around the horse's neck, but do untie the rope so that if the horse pulls back his neck is not damaged. Alternatively, leave the headcollar on but still untie the rope.

If it's cold consider washing the legs after a rug has been put on, taking care not to soak the rug. Towel-drying some areas also allows the horse to dry quicker. If you're lucky enough to have a solarium you don't need to worry about the horse becoming chilled, and besides drying off, they have health benefits including reducing stiffness after work and promoting recovery and relaxation.

The sweat scraper will remove any excess water.

The feet and shoes

As a general rule, a horse needs to be trimmed or shod every 6–8 weeks. However, not all horses are the same so discuss the horse's individual needs with the farrier. As you pick out the feet daily, it is a good idea to monitor them (and the shoes if the horse has them) to gauge when they need to be trimmed and/or shoes refitted. The most obvious sign is a missing shoe but a clanking/abnormal sound when the horse moves tells you one is loose, and the shoe might move visibly when the horse's weight is taken off it. Other warning signs are shown in the accompanying photos.

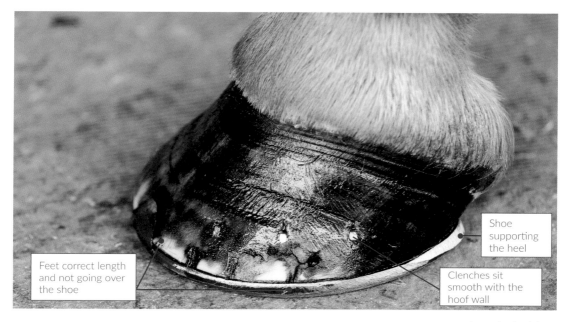

Shoe supporting the heel

Feet correct length and not going over the shoe

Clenches sit smooth with the hoof wall

A newly shod foot.

A newly trimmed and shod foot gives a good baseline for monitoring the feet. The picture above shows a newly shod foot and if compared to the picture below, demonstrates the differences that will develop over the time between visits by the farrier.

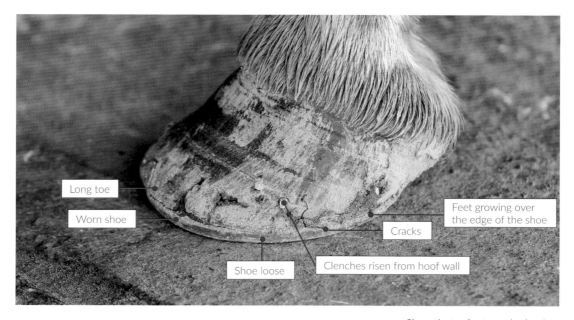

Long toe

Worn shoe

Feet growing over the edge of the shoe

Cracks

Shoe loose

Clenches risen from hoof wall

Signs that a foot needs shoeing.

Recognising when the feet of an unshod horse needs attention is a different skill. You still need to look at the length of the hoof, paying particular attention to the length of the toes as long toes puts pressure on the underlying structures of the leg. As the unshod hoof is in direct contact with the ground, the edge may wear more than when shod. If it is wearing unevenly, or cracks, splits or bulging areas appear, it's time to call the farrier.

Hooves in need of attention.

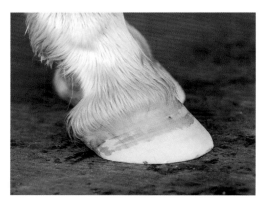

Newly trimmed hooves.

Summary

- Reasons for grooming — improves appearance, keeps skin healthy, aids circulation and muscle tone, builds horse-human relationship, opportunity to check for injuries.

- Key items — hoofpick, dandy brush, body brush, curry comb (rubber, plastic, metal), mane comb/brush, sponges, water brush, cloth.

- When choosing which item to use — consider appropriateness for the body part, the horse's preferences, whether the horse is clipped, time of year.

- Be safe — think where you are: is the horse tied up, have you got room to move safely around the horse?

- Be efficient — put effort into every brushstroke; groom with clean brushes.

- Ideally thorough groom every day, but a quick groom will do when time is short.

- Picking out feet is very important — should be done at least once a day, in heel to toe direction, paying particular attention to areas where dirt/stones could get trapped.

- Think about time of year — if it is cold don't remove the rug completely.

- Brush/wash off after work — particularly where tack has been, e.g. saddle, girth area, around the ears, under boots.

- Signs a horse needs to see the farrier — lost or loose shoe, risen clenches, long foot, overgrown foot, cracked foot, uneven wear on foot.

TRAINING TIPS

1. Visit tack shops or look online to become familiar with the various types of grooming kit available; try to work out how and when you might use them.

2. Practise grooming a variety of horses with different brushes.

3. Spend time getting to know the horses you work with, know what their body looks and feels like normally.

4. Watch a farrier at work, to see the 'before and after' hooves for a variety of horses.

5. Have a look at horses on your yard — try to identify the ones you think are ready to be seen by the farrier, then check back with the owner/yard manager to see if you are right.

Chapter 9

Rugs for Horses

Rugs for Horses

Most horses and ponies will, at some point, have a rug on, and some horses seem to have many different rugs for different occasions. Some horses may just have a rain sheet, and others a really warm stable or turnout rug. The most important thing to remember is that every horse's needs are different. Make sure you think about why a horse needs the rug, and then make sure it fits well. There are many different types of rug available and designs are advancing all the time. The main function of a rug is to keep the horse warm and dry, but how they do this may vary. Likewise, other types of rug are available, for example to protect against flies.

Choosing a rug

Rugs, like clothes, come in different standard sizes, but the shape and fit will vary depending on the brand. In the UK, rugs are measured in feet and inches, with the measurement taken from the centre of the horse's chest to the point of the horse's buttock. European rugs are measured in centimetres and refer to the measurement from the top of the horse's withers along the spine to the top of the tail.

The line indicates where to measure for a rug, from the centre of the horse's chest to the point of buttock

How to measure a horse for a rug.

Rug sizes in the UK are still measured for length imperially and come in 3in (7.5cm) increments, starting at around 3ft (91cm) and going up to over 7ft (2.13m) in length. Different brands suit different types of horses and, as with human clothing, finding the rug that fits a horse best can be a matter of trial and error, especially if the horse is wide-chested or very narrow. We then face further decisions about the weight of the rug and the strength of the outer material. The weight is related to the amount of filling in the lining. As a rough guide, up to 100g (about 3.5oz) could be considered a lightweight rug; over 300g (about 10.5oz) heavyweight, and medium weight covers everything in between. The outer material is measured in denier (D) and relates to the number of yarns used to make one thread e.g. 600D. The higher the number, the more hard-wearing the outer shell is. If you have a horse who has a habit of tearing rugs you may want to look for one with a high denier and with a rip-stop or ballistic outer material (which will have reinforced threads running through it) making the outer shell very resilient.

Styles of rug

A standard rug is a traditionally shaped design, which leaves the neck uncovered. It might, however, have fastenings to which a neck cover can be attached.

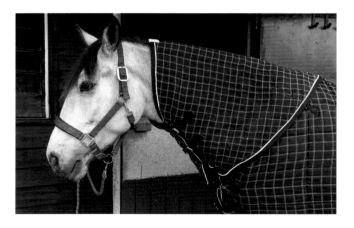

A detachable neck cover, attached with Velcro or clip fastenings, is useful with lighter weight rugs as it can be removed for spells of warmer weather.

A high-neck rug sits in front of the withers and covers part way up the neck. This type of rug offers more protection than a standard neck rug but not as much as a full neck cover. Sometimes this shape of rug is used to stop the horse's mane being rubbed, as can happen with the traditionally shaped rug.

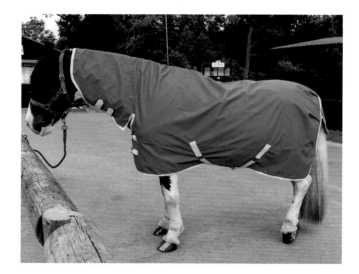

A full-neck or combo rug has the neck cover integrated into the design. This is a common feature with turnout rugs as it makes it very warm and there are fewer seams into which water can leak. This style is often used when a horse is fully clipped or has a very fine coat.

All the types of rugs pictured will have various fittings to keep them in place. These could consist of buckles or clips at the front of the rug and leg straps or a fillet string at the back. Leg straps pass between the hind legs, cross through each other and fasten on the inside of the rug near the stifle, and behind the hindquarters to help prevent the rug blowing forwards over the horse's back. They also keep the rug from slipping round, which can be especially useful when the horse is playing or rolling in the field. A fillet string is made from soft plaited cord and sits under the tail; it stops the rug from slipping forwards and is more commonly found on stable rugs and coolers.

There are usually two surcingles or belly straps that cross over underneath the horse to secure the middle of the rug. These straps keep the rug on and in the right place.

Choosing the right weight of rug

With so much choice it can be difficult to select the best type and weight of rug to keep the horse warm without becoming overheated. For a horse, wearing too many rugs can cause as big a problem as not wearing enough, although not everyone realises this.

The air temperature will help you choose which rug to use and, although it might sound obvious, it is wise to keep checking the temperature throughout the day, especially in the spring or autumn months when the mornings can start off cold but then get hotter. It is easy for the horse to overheat in this situation if he has been turned out in a heavyweight rug. If the horse has to wear one rug all day, then pick the rug for the warmest part of the day rather than the coldest. Remember, a horse can move around and eat to keep warm but cannot take a layer off to cool down.

Some horses are naturally tougher than others. Although there can be exceptions, a native pony is likely to cope with the colder weather by growing a thick coat quicker than a fine-haired, thin-skinned horse such as a Thoroughbred. Some horses are naturally 'warm' and might not require a heavy rug, whereas others (e.g. older horses) may feel the cold easily.

It is also important to consider the horse's body weight, age and general health. A horse who is underweight will struggle to gain weight if he is cold. Likewise, a fat pony left naked will burn more calories keeping warm than if you put on a warm rug. An older or ill horse may feel the cold more than a younger, healthy horse and may appreciate some extra protection. Remember, every horse is an individual and it is important to take the time to work out their needs based on all the factors mentioned.

Native ponies have developed to grow a thick coat to protect them from the weather.

Types of rug

Stable rugs

A stable rug is a quilted type used indoors. It can be made from fabrics that are designed to be 'breathable', which means that moisture is drawn away from the horse's skin. A stable rug tends to be less bulky than a turnout rug. When choosing which weight to use think about the position of the stable in relation to the predominant wind direction or any draughts that might affect the horse (stables positioned at the end of the barn next to the doors can often be very draughty and cold compared to those in the middle of the row).

An example of a stable rug.

Turnout rugs

Turnout rugs range from rain sheets with no filling, that keep the drizzle off, to heavyweight protection from the coldest weather. You should ideally choose the lightest weight needed, especially if you are not able to swap the rug during the day when the temperature could rise.

Turnout rugs are breathable, with a waterproof outer layer and tend to be fitted slightly deeper than a stable rug to help protect the horse from the weather. You may have noticed that horses tend to stand with their backs to the wind or heavy rain; this is why turnout rugs are designed with long tail flaps to keep the wind from blowing up the back of the rug.

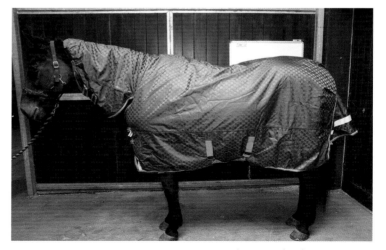

An example of a turnout rug.

Cooler rugs

A cooler rug is one of the most versatile rugs you will come across; there is one for nearly every occasion. They are made from a variety of fabrics such as cotton, fleece or mesh, and are lightweight. Fleece and mesh coolers have wicking properties that allow the air to circulate under the rug while the fibres draw the moisture through the rug, away from the horse's skin, to the surface where it evaporates, leaving the horse warm and dry underneath. This makes them ideal to use after the horse has been washed-off, bathed, or after exercise in the winter while they are still a little too warm to have their stable rugs on. A fleece cooler can also be used as a lightweight stable rug on an unclipped horse (although bedding sticks badly to some coolers).

Sometimes a fleece rug can stretch over time; therefore it is important that the fit of the rug is checked regularly to prevent pressure points and rubs over the horse's shoulders and withers.

An example of a cooler rug.

Fly rugs

These lightweight rugs are made from close-weave nylon or polyester material, designed to be tough enough to protect the horse from being bitten by insects or annoyed by flies in the spring/summer months but cool enough to stop the horse overheating. They tend to be closely fitted around the neck and belly compared to other rugs to prevent flies from getting underneath. They usually have a full-neck cover that comes up to or over the horse's ears, with an elasticated cuff to keep it close to the back of the head, a long tail flap and a long belly flap that wraps underneath the horse. As well as protection from flies, these rugs often offer protection from the sun, helping to keep the horse cool and stop the coat colour fading. Some fly rugs now also have a waterproof section along the back, offering some protection from rain showers but without being as warm as a full rain sheet.

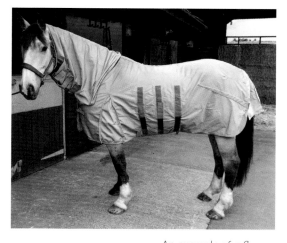

An example of a fly rug.

Putting on and taking off a rug

There are no hard-and-fast rules about the order in which you do up the straps on your horse's rug. The routine you choose should be based on your and the horse's safety and may change dependent on the situation. Some simple facts to remember are:

- Rugs naturally want to slide backwards unless they are done up at the front.

- Anything fastened only around a horse's middle can cause them to panic and buck if they get loose.

- Leg straps still done up but slipped down the hind legs can trigger a really frightening situation as a horse's instinct is to panic and kick out at something wrapped round his lower legs.

- If rugging up outside, wind may cause the rug to blow or make it harder to keep the rug in position.

Putting on a rug

To put on a rug, first make sure that the horse is tied up in a safe area. If you have to put the rug on in a field always put a headcollar on the horse and ask someone to hold him for you if possible. If no one is available use somewhere such as a field shelter to reduce the risk of the horse taking off round the field before the rug is properly secured. If a loose rug becomes tangled in the horse's legs it can frighten and injure the horse as well as ripping the rug. Even the quietest, most sensible horse can be alarmed at something unexpected, like a person suddenly appearing around a hedge, and it is just not worth the risk of injuring you or him; always be safe.

You should tie up the belly straps and ensure that the leg straps are fastened to the D-rings before the rug goes on. Otherwise there is a risk of them swinging and hitting you, the horse or something else as the rug is swung over the horse's back (it is really easy for them to wrap round something and get stuck). Also, you do not want the horse to become nervous and tense every time a rug is put on because he is anticipating being hit with a loose strap.

A safe procedure for rugging is outlined below. If you are unsure of how the horse will react to it (for example, a horse you have never handled before) it is best to follow the safest procedure possible.

Folding the rug makes it easier to pick up and handle, especially if it is thick/heavy or has a neck cover.

Aim to place the rug over the withers. How you do this will depend on your height and how big the horse is. Stand on the left side of the horse next to his shoulder. If you are tall enough, lift the rug up and place it over the withers gently. If not, gently throw the edge of the rug over the withers; you can then slide the rest of the rug up and over into position.

Be careful of launching the whole rug into the air, especially if the horse is nervous or new to being rugged. In these situations it is best to use the folding method to minimise the chance of frightening him.

Once on, unfold the rug, making sure it is sitting a little further forward than where you want it to end up — this way, if the horse moves and it slides back a little, it's still easy to work with. Then do up the chest straps, pull the rug back into position and fasten the rest of the straps. If the rug does slip too far back, undo the straps, remove it and then put it on again. This ensures that the horse's hair is lying flat against the skin and is comfortable for the horse. Pulling a rug against the direction of the coat is quite hard to do, besides being unpleasant for the horse.

Putting on a rug

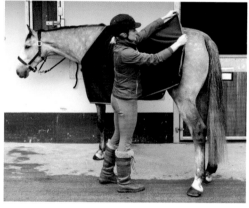

Place the rug over the horse's back.

Unfold the rug and fasten up the straps. It does not matter which order the straps are fastened up in.

Taking off a rug

When taking the rug off, always check for legs straps first (if you do not spot them you can get into a really tricky and dangerous situation with them wrapped around the horse's fetlocks). If the rug has them, unfasten them carefully (do not let them drop down between the legs and bang the hocks), and re-clip them back to the rug on the outside of the legs, to keep them out of the way. Undo any surcingles then, if the rug has a neck cover, undo it and fold it out of the way before undoing the chest fastenings. Once all of the straps are undone, fold the front of the rug backwards before sliding the folded rug off over the tail.

Fold the rug neatly and hang it up out of the way. You could tie up the belly straps now, ready for the rug to be put on again.

Taking off a rug

Undo all the straps and fold the rug from front to back.

Slide the rug off the horse's back and then hang it up neatly.

Check the fit of a rug

Having a rug that fits the horse well is essential to keep the horse comfortable and protected. Try to get into the habit of checking the fit of a rug every time you put one on, as the straps can stretch over time and may need adjusting.

It is easy to pick up the wrong rug so check it fits as follows:

- The front of the rug over the chest should have an overlap of fabric so it does not rub or roll back.

- The rug should sit well forward in front of the withers so as not to rub (it will naturally slide back as the horse moves).

- There should be room to fit a flat hand comfortably between the rug and the horse all the way round the neck and shoulders.

- The rug should be the right length to fully cover the horse from the withers to the top of the tail.

- The rug should be deep enough to reach beneath the horse's body; you should not be able to see any of the horse's body protruding from underneath the rug when looking at the horse from the side.

The belly straps should be adjusted so that you can fit a hand in between the centre of the horse's belly and the cross of the straps. This allows the horse to move and roll without restriction and keeps the rug in position.

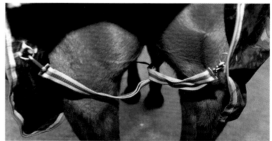

The leg straps are fastened around each hind leg, with one strap going through the centre of the other to make a figure of eight shape. The straps should sit roughly a hand's distance from the horse's leg to allow him to move comfortably.

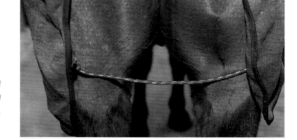

If the rug has a fillet string this should sit underneath the tail with enough room for a hand to fit between the horse and the string.

In general, rugs that do not fit properly will cause rubs, sores, pressure points, restrict the horse's movement or, at best, just not do the job they are meant for. Always think about the horse's comfort and safety when fitting one.

Summary

- The main function of a rug is to keep the horse warm and dry.

- There are various styles, such as standard neck, high-neck and full-neck and indoor and outdoor.

- When choosing a rug, consider each horse's individual needs and requirements.

- Consider the air temperature, time of year, age of horse, body weight, general health of the horse.

- When putting the rug on there is no specific order in which to fasten the straps, but you must consider your safety and that of the horse.

- Dangers to consider: rugs naturally want to slide backwards; wind can cause rugs to blow back up over the horse; straps caught round the middle of a horse, or leg straps caught around the bottom of a horse's legs can both cause the horse to panic.

- Aim to place the rug over the horse's back rather than throw it.

- Fold the rug back in the direction of the horse's hair.

- When taking the rug off, always check for leg straps!

- Fold the rug back and slide back over the tail.

- The rug needs to fit well to prevent discomfort.

- The rug should sit well forward of the withers, be long enough to fully cover the horse, be deep enough to sit below the horse's body.

- Leg straps should thread through each other and you should be able to fit one hand between the horse's leg and strap.

- You should be able to fit a fist between the horse and the straps.

- You should be able to fit one hand between horse and fillet string.

TRAINING TIPS

1. Visit tack shops or look online to become familiar with the huge variety of rugs available. Find out all the information on them, such as variations in material, weight, denier, styles.

2. Look at rugs on horses and see how they fit, good and bad points, how the shape suits the type of horse. Ask the owner questions about the rugs they use and why they use them.

3. Practise handling rugs — folding them up and carrying them, practise the actions for putting them on by throwing them over a gate.

Chapter 10

Field Care

Field suitability

Daily field checks

Summary

Field Care

Horses usually appreciate having access to as much turnout as possible, but they need a safe area that meets their needs.

Once a field has been deemed suitable for horses, it still needs checking daily to ensure it remains safe, properly maintained and has food, water and shelter. Ideally these checks should be made in the morning before any horses are turned out. This is not always practical on a busy yard and it may be more efficient to make checks by walking around the field when you turn the first horses out. There will be times, e.g. after storms/high winds and around firework season, when more frequent checks are needed, and before any horses are turned out. It is increasingly common for people to let off fireworks in rural areas, near equestrian facilities, and firework debris may land in your fields; similarly, storms may blow trees or branches down, which could damage your fencing.

Field suitability

Before you can thoroughly check a field, you first need to think about what makes a good, safe field for horses.

Fencing

There are many different types of fencing suitable for horses, but some are only suitable for other farm animals and can be dangerous to horses. Fences should be strong and high enough to prevent horses from escaping: a rough height guide is 1.1–1.4m (43–55in) for horses and 1–1.3m (39–51in) for ponies.

Types of fencing and their suitability

Type of fence	Suitable for use with horses?
Post and rail (plastic or wood)	Yes
Electric rope or tape (either on permanent fence posts or temporary plastic ones)	Yes — best if double strand used to make it easier for the horses to see

Type of fence	Suitable for use with horses?
Cattle wire (thin electric wire, single strand with temporary posts)	No — not easily visible as wire is very thin and disappears into background, thus easy for horses to run into and become injured
Barbed wire	No — can injure and damage rugs; horses tend to try to lean over it to graze when grass is limited in the winter
Sheep/pig netting	No — horse can get foot/shoe caught in the squares, causing serious damage
Plain wire	No — not easy to see; horses may run into it and be injured
Wall	Yes — but must be high enough to discourage jumping out
Hedge	Yes — but must not contain poisonous shrubs/trees and must be solid enough to prevent horses squeezing out

Some examples of suitable fencing (i) post and rail, (ii) electric and (iii) hedge.

Some examples of unsuitable fencing (i) barbed wire and (ii) barbed wire and sheep netting.

Ground and grass

Ground quality and grass coverage will vary over the course of a year, but it is weather extremes that potentially cause problems. Very wet and boggy ground leads to excessive poaching (broken up, slushy ground caused by the horses moving around) and increases the risk of lost shoes and injury. A field ruined by excessive poaching will take a long time to recover. Quite often, yards will have winter and summer paddocks, to give fields time to rest after use. It can be dangerous to turn horses out into long, rich grass, as it may contain extremely high levels of sugar. This sudden change in diet can cause colic or a sudden weight increase. Conversely, a field with barely any grass coverage won't furnish the horses with what they need, resulting in weight loss and, potentially, fighting between horses looking for food.

Horses tend to avoid grazing areas strewn with weeds (e.g. nettles or docks), resulting in patches of long grass that are of no use. Similarly if there is excessive droppings, you will see areas of long grass develop around the patches of droppings (with the grass becoming sour), and areas of short grass where the horses continue to graze.

A good field will have short but even grass coverage and be free of weeds and droppings.

Usage

The recommended ratio is a minimum of 0.6 hectare (1.5 acres) of grazing land per horse. Too many horses per acreage will result in over-grazing, leaving the field unable to provide adequate nutrition for the horses without additional hay or haylage. Too few horses and the grass could become overly long and the residents overly heavy. Where paddocks are of a manageable size, droppings should be removed daily in order to reduce the spread of equine parasites (worms). If the field is regularly cleared of droppings and has weeds removed, the grass will be more evenly grazed and patches of long and short grass will be avoided.

Shelter

No matter what the time of year, horses need some form of shelter, either from wind, rain and snow in winter, or from the sun and flies in summer (as well as unseasonal weather). Shelter can range from the natural (hedges and trees) to man-made solutions (wooden field shelters, walls and rugs).

Daily field checks

When checking the field, think from both a safety and a welfare perspective: what will keep the horses safe, and what do they need while in the field? Try to weigh up the potential risk each feature poses to the horses and consider how can you minimise or remove that risk. It is important to report any damage or deterioration quickly, before the problem becomes too big.

Gate

A sensible place to start is the entrance gate. This needs to be easy to open, close securely and swing so that you can enter and leave the field safely with a horse, without being squashed or letting other horses escape in the process.

Fencing

Walk around the fence line to check that there are no broken rails or posts and that everything looks safe. If the fence is electric, check that it is still working. The energiser usually has a built-in light that flashes with the electric pulses to tell you it is working. Check that none of the tape has come loose or is touching the floor as this will short out the electricity. If you hear any clicking this is a good indication the fence is shorting out somewhere. Electric fencing using temporary posts often needs day-to-day maintenance. The posts lean easily, particularly when the ground is softer, the tape may become loose and, if it is powered by a battery, this will need regular recharging.

As you are walking around the fence line, you can also check that the ground is not excessively wet/boggy, look for any hazards (litter, holes, fallen trees/branches) and check for any poisonous plants or trees (see below).

Poisonous plants and trees

The most common poisonous plants and trees to look out for in the UK are shown below.

Ragwort

Ragwort is a highly poisonous plant that is very resilient. You will easily recognise it by its bright yellow flowers (see following pictures). It is not normally eaten by horses, but if there is not a

Ragwort at the rosette stage.

Ragwort at the flowering stage.

Make sure you get the roots as well when digging up ragwort.

lot of grass, or if the ragwort has been cut and dried (e.g. during hay-making), horses may eat it. By law you must remove ragwort, including the roots, from your land, but as it also poisonous to humans, you must wear protective gloves when handling it.

Foxglove

Foxglove, also known as digitalis, is highly poisonous to horses and humans. It is easily recognised by its bell-shape flowers on a tall, tubular stem, growing up to 2m (6ft 6in) tall. The most common foxglove has purple flowers, but different species have different coloured flowers (e.g. white, yellow). It flowers throughout the summer months, and is most commonly found in shadier areas such as woodland, moorland and hedgerows.

The common foxglove.

Sycamore

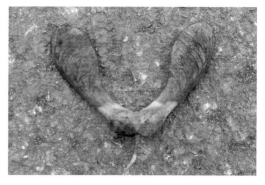

You will easily recognise a sycamore tree by its 'helicopter seeds'. Sycamore poisoning causes a disorder called seasonal pasture myopathy, which most commonly occurs in the autumn or spring. If you have sycamore trees where your horse is grazing, it is best to fence off the area where the seeds and leaves fall.

Sycamore seeds.

Oak

The acorns, buds, leaves and blossom of an oak tree can all be toxic to horses. This tree is easily recognised by its acorns and its leaves, which tend to have seven to nine lobes. Oak poisoning in horses is not very common, but if an oak tree is present in a grazing field, it is best either to remove it or fence if off. Acorns are more of a problem when they fall to the ground in the autumn, but they are also particularly toxic when still green. After high winds or storms, there will be more leaves and acorns on the ground, so it is particularly important to remove these from any grazing pasture, as well as any fallen branches.

The oak tree's leaves and acorn.

Yew

The yew tree is extremely poisonous and can often cause death almost instantly. This evergreen shrub or tree has distinctive needle-like but soft, flat leaves that have a dark green upper surface and paler green underside. Yew is common in churchyards so you should check any fields that are next to a churchyard and fence off areas that your horse could reach.

Yew has distinctive needle-like leaves and red seed coverings.

The need for checks and control

Regular checks need to be made of the field as well as surrounding areas. Poisonous plants or trees should always be removed or fenced off where possible. When there is less grass available the horse is more likely to eat poisonous plants that have not been removed, so by giving supplementary hay and not overstocking the field, the risk can be minimised.

Water

Whatever the water source in the field — trough, stream, or automatic drinker — check that it is providing clean, fresh water. Some troughs may refill automatically but it's important to check that the water is flowing and that the trough or supply pipe hasn't broken or frozen up. Other troughs may need to refilled by hand, and the water level must be checked daily. Any trough must be emptied and scrubbed clean regularly. In winter, you may need to break and remove ice from the surface every morning and evening. If a stream is the source of water, check for any debris or obvious signs of pollution, and that the horse can still gain access to it.

Summary

- The field needs to be checked daily for safety and for the welfare of the horses.

- Key areas to check — gate, fencing, ground conditions, hazards, poisonous plants, water supply.

- Jobs to be done daily — remove droppings.

- Jobs to be done weekly — cleaning water troughs.

- Key problems that make a field unsuitable for horses — unsuitable or broken fencing, excessively poached ground, overstocking, excessive droppings, weeds, no shelter.

TRAINING TIPS

1. Practise checking a variety of fields at different times of year.

2. Walk along a footpath or out in the countryside and look at fields and fencing as you go. You will see a huge variety of methods in use; try to decide whether the field would be suitable for horses or not.

3. Get into the habit of paying attention every time you are in the field. Even if it is not officially 'field check' time, vigilance may prevent an accident or injury.

Chapter 11

Tacking Up a Horse

Tacking Up a Horse

Tacking up can seem complicated at first, but with practice and patience it will become second nature. At some point, every learner manages to get the noseband in the horse's mouth, watches the bridle slide off over the ears or gets the numnah the wrong way up. The aim is to put the tack on efficiently while being mindful of the horse's comfort.

Before you begin, check that you have the right items. Tack sometimes finds its way on to the wrong peg (especially in a busy riding school where clients might untack) so alarm bells should ring if you pick up a small saddle for a large horse. Once you have the correct tack, hook the bridle (and reins) over your shoulder and slide the same arm through the gullet of the saddle so it sits in the crook of your elbow. Boots can be placed on the saddle, leaving a hand free to open doors and gates. Put the tack down near the stable or tie up area, where it will be easy to reach but cannot be reached by the horse.

Ideally, there will be a fold-out saddle rack outside each stable, but you may need to improvise. The door of an empty stable makes a good saddle rack (make sure the saddle is balanced safely) or you might have to set it down on the floor. In this case, put the numnah down first and place the girth between the back of the saddle and the wall to prevent scratching the leather. Try to find a hook for the bridle, although laying it over the back of the saddle will do if needs must. If you put the saddle on your own stable door, make sure the horse cannot reach it; tie him up first. Saddles, in particular, are expensive and a careless knock can cause an unsightly scratch that devalues it, or may even damage it seriously.

The order of tacking up depends on the situation. If you have a running martingale attached to the reins, put the bridle on first as the girth will need threading through the martingale loop in due course. In winter, especially with a clipped horse, keep the rug on for as long as possible, folding it over the quarters while you put the saddle on. If the horse isn't needed straight away, put the rug back over the saddle, loosely doing up the chest straps and surcingles (with the leg straps neatly hooked away from the legs).

The bridle

Parts of the bridle

All the parts of the bridle are identified in the image on the right.

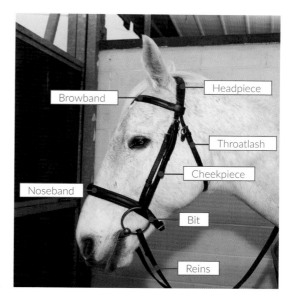

Parts of the bridle.

Putting on a bridle with a cavesson noseband

First, tie the horse up. Hold the bridle up by the headpiece. Check that the noseband and throatlash are undone and that the noseband, cheekpieces and bit are not twisted and the straps are lying flat.

i.   *Place the reins over the horse's head, then unfasten the headcollar and buckle it round the horse's neck in the same way you would do when grooming the head. Undo the lead rope but leave the rope threaded through the tie-string.*

ii. *Staying to the left of the horse, position yourself by his head, facing forwards, and hold the bridle halfway up the cheekpieces. If the horse moves his head you can put your right arm around the nose to steady it. Place the bit flat on your hand and raise it to the horse's lips. Some horses may take a moment to open their mouth, so be patient and allow them time. Trying to push the bit in will be uncomfortable for the horse and create more resistance. If the horse does not automatically open his mouth, slide your thumb gently into the corner of the lips, where there are no teeth, to encourage him to do so. Be careful not to hit the teeth with the bit as you put it in.*

iii. As you slide the bit in, lift the bridle towards the ears to keep the bit high enough to stay in the mouth, taking care not to catch the eyes with the cheekpieces. This is the part most people struggle with initially — it takes practice.

iv. Gently bend the horse's ears to slip them between the headpiece and the browband, taking care not to let the bridle slide back down the face. The headpiece should sit comfortably behind both ears.

v. Comfort is paramount. Check that the top of the mane is lying flat under the headpiece and lift the forelock from under the browband. Make sure the browband is level from the front and does not press on the base of the ears at the sides. Next, check the bit is the same height on either side and sitting evenly in the mouth. The noseband should sit level, with the side straps in line with the cheekpieces, clear of the eyes.

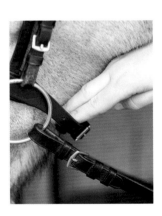

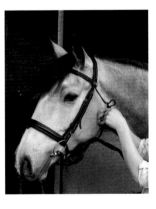

vi. When fastened, there should be room for two fingers between the cavesson noseband and the bony part of the horse's jaw.

vii. Make sure the throatlash is not twisted through the cheekpiece on the offside when you fasten it, and allow four fingers between it and the cheek.

viii. If you need to leave the horse tacked and tied up, twist the reins over each other, thread the throatlash through them and fasten, to keep them safely out of the way. The headcollar can then be placed back over the bridle; you might need to expand it to do so. Don't forget to re-tie the lead rope.

Different nosebands

Sometimes, patterns of noseband other than a cavesson may be fitted. These are used to help control a horse who opens his mouth or crosses his jaw. They should be fitted as follows:

Drop noseband — *The lower straps of a drop noseband should sit below the bit, passing round the back to sit in the chin groove. There should be enough room to fit one finger between the noseband and the bony part of the jaw. Be careful not to trap muzzle hair in the buckle.*

Flash noseband — *The top part of this noseband should fit a little tighter (not too much) than a normal cavesson to stop it pulling down on to the soft part of the nose, where it might interfere with breathing. You should always be able to place one finger between the bony part of the jaw or the nose and the leather. The lower strap (flash strap) should pass below the bit and sit in the chin groove, again with room for one finger. Position the buckle of this strap on the soft part above the nostril.*

Running martingale

A running martingale is designed to prevent the horse from escaping your control by lifting his head up. It places downward pressure on the reins and, as a result, the bit and horse's mouth, when the head is raised too high. If fitted properly it does nothing when the horse is working correctly, only coming into action when needed. Often the rings are left threaded through the reins and the martingale taken on and off as part of the bridle. The neckstrap is placed over the head and the girth threads through the lower strap.

The martingale should only come into action when the horse's head is too high. To check fit, see overleaf. To confirm that the short straps of the martingale are roughly the correct length, take both rings to one side of the neck; the rings should reach just below the withers or under the throat when pulled tight.

The neck strap holds the lower martingale strap in position

The rings run along the reins and put downward pressure on the reins when the head is raised

The short straps that attach to the reins must be free from any twists

Rubber or leather 'rein stops' prevents the reins from sliding too far forward and becoming tangled in the billets, buckles or bit rings

A rubber stop can be fitted between the neck strap and the lower strap to hold them in position

The girth is threaded through a loop in the lower strap

A running martingale.

The lowest point of the neckstrap should sit at the base of the neck and you should be able to fit four fingers between it and the withers.

The lower martingale strap can be adjusted by the buckle that sits in front of the girth. You should be able to fit four fingers between it and the horse's chest.

The saddle

Parts of a saddle

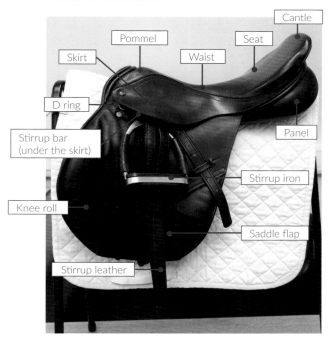 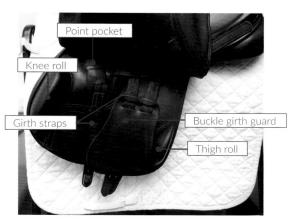

Parts of a saddle.

Fitting a saddle

Before you pick up the saddle, check whether the numnah and girth are already attached. If the girth is detached you might want to place it over your shoulder or leave it on the stable door to free up your hands. If you drape it over the saddle it may fall off while the saddle is being lifted on to the horse. If the numnah is detached, put this on the horse first; otherwise, put the saddle with attached numnah on the horse's back a little forward of where it will eventually sit, and gently slide it back, smoothing the hair in the right direction. Try to lower it gently. Make sure the numnah is properly strapped on, level, with no parts wrinkled under the saddle. Then lift the front up into the saddle's gullet to give space above the withers. It is important you use the numnah that has been assigned to this horse. A certain horse's saddle may require a specific numnah (or, in some cases, other forms of padding) to ensure a good fit, and the wrong type or thickness could cause discomfort. Numnahs come in many styles and may be designed to attach to girth straps or D-rings and the girth. Make sure all are done up neatly.

Once everything is in place, do up the girth. If not already attached, do up the offside on one of the lower holes until you know how much room you will have to tighten it on the other side. If the girth has elastic inserts then buckle this side on first; otherwise it is easy to over-tighten the girth by over-stretching the elastic. Normally you should use the first and third girth straps (unless there are only two). This is a safety measure as the first and second straps normally extend from the same piece of webbing; if this breaks, the girth will still be secured by the third girth strap, which is attached to a separate piece. Some saddles have extra girth straps; let the buckle marks be your guide as to what works best for each particular horse.

If the girth is already attached to the saddle, unfold it carefully so it does not bang the horse's leg or elbow as it drops. Remember, it only needs to be tight enough to keep the saddle in position until the rider is ready to mount. As a rough guide you should be able to slide the flat of your hand comfortably between the horse and the girth. If you can pull the girth away from the horse's side, it is probably too loose.

The horse will appreciate your doing the girth gradually, particularly if he is sensitive. Face the front so you can pay attention to the horse's expression while you tighten the girth so you can base your approach on his response. Aim to have the girth at a similar height/hole on both sides. If you're short of holes and the girth is still loose you will need a shorter one.

Buckle guards should be pulled down on both sides over the buckles; these protect the saddle flap from wear. The girth will naturally loosen as it warms up and the horse gets moving, so it will need to be tightened just before the rider gets on.

The saddle should sit just behind the withers. As a guide, when the girth hangs it should sit about 5cm (2in) behind the elbow. Make sure the front of the numnah is lifted away from the withers to avoid pressure and pain for the horse. If the numnah has attachments these should be done up to prevent it from slipping when the horse is ridden.

Normally the girth will be fastened up on the first and third girth straps. Attach it to the offside first, making sure it is threaded through the strap on the numnah, and fasten it on the first or second hole; it can be tightened up later. Make sure you use the same straps on each side.

Untacking

The order in which you remove the saddle and bridle will depend on whether you have a martingale or not. If the horse is wearing a martingale, take the saddle off first to release the lower martingale strap from the girth. Once removed, put the tack somewhere it can't be damaged until you can return it to the tack room. If the numnah is sweaty, remove it and hang it up to air, or put it in the washing pile. Bits should be rinsed off to remove any saliva and food. It is important to hang tack up correctly so that the leather or fabric does not stretch or become out of shape. After untacking, the horse should be checked over for injuries, washed or brushed off and rugged up as appropriate.

Taking off the saddle

Removing the saddle is easy; just reverse the saddling up procedure. Always consider the horse's comfort and avoid damage to tack.

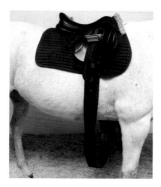

i. Undo the girth on the nearside, remembering, if a martingale has been used, to unthread it from the girth.

ii. Let the girth hang, being careful not to let it bang the horse's leg.

iii. Duck under the neck to the other side and either undo the girth completely, or leave it attached and drape it over the top of the saddle as shown.

iv. Slip one hand under the pommel and grasp the cantle with the other, making sure you have hold of the pads too. Lift the saddle off the horse's back slightly before pulling it towards you, trying not to drag it.

Taking off the bridle

This is slightly easier than putting it on, provided you undo the correct straps. The most common mistake is to unbuckle a cheekpiece, so the bit falls out of the mouth, leaving the rest of the bridle still fastened. Don't unbuckle straps attached to the bit, but start by putting the headcollar round the horse's neck, with the lead rope untied but sitting through the tie-string (move the reins and martingale neckstrap up the neck a little so the headcollar sits behind them).

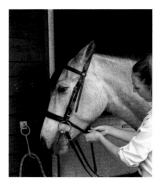

i. Start by undoing the throatlash and the noseband.

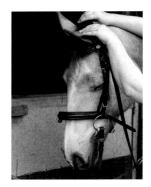

ii. Slide the reins (and martingale neckstrap if there is one) up the neck to the headpiece behind the horse's ears. Standing to the nearside of the horse, facing slightly forwards, hold the headpiece, reins and martingale neckstrap together and gently slip the bridle forwards over the ears.

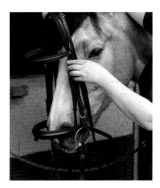

iii. Wait for the horse to drop the bit from his mouth; if you pull it out it will bang the teeth.

Put the bridle over your shoulder while you refasten the headcollar properly and re-tie the lead rope. To keep the bridle tidy and easier to carry, loop the reins, martingale neckstrap and the girth loop through the throatlash, then wrap the noseband round the bridle and buckle loosely.

Tying the bridle up for storage keeps it neat and tidy and makes it easier to handle the next time it is needed.

Brushing boots

Brushing boots come in many styles, shapes and colours and are used for everything from riding to turning out. They are designed to protect the horse's lower leg.

Generally, hind boots are longer and wider than front boots and they might have an extra strap. The strike pad sits on the inside of the leg, with the widest part over the fetlock, and the fastenings on the outside. Normally, if the boot has a single Velcro closure it will close towards the back of the leg. However, some boots have two straps, with one of them closing forwards. If in doubt, ask someone more experienced. The strike pad on the inside should cover from the bottom of the fetlock to just below the knee or hock. They shouldn't be so long that they press on the bottom of the knee or hock.

When removed, brushing boots may need rinsing and hanging up to dry. Alternatively you may be able just to brush off any arena surface before pairing them up and strapping them shut.

 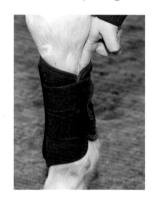 

i. With the strike pad to the inside of the leg, slide the boot down from the knee or hock so the hair lies smoothly, and stop when the widest part of the strike pad covers the fetlock. Make sure all the fabric lies flat, without wrinkles.

ii. The boot should be fastened tight enough to prevent it from slipping down but not so tight that it interferes with circulation. You should be able to fit a finger comfortably in the top.

iii. Clean boots paired up for storage.

The importance of correctly fitting tack

Checking tack for comfort every time you tack up is an essential habit. It is easy to overlook small changes in behaviour if you are tacking up the same horse every day, only realising something is wrong when the horse lets you know in a very obvious way that he is uncomfortable (biting, kicking, etc.). If a normally quiet horse exhibits signs of grumpiness or discomfort as he is tacked up, take notice and seek advice.

Just as you would not walk comfortably with a pebble in your shoe, an uncomfortable horse, whose numnah is tucked up cannot perform to the best of his ability.

When you first learn to tack up you will normally be given tack that fits. However, it is easy to fetch the wrong item or find that a bridle has been used on another horse and readjusted. In such cases, you need a rough idea of how a saddle and bridle fit correctly. If you are not sure that they do, ask for advice.

Browband — Ideally you should be able to fit two fingers between the middle of the horse's head and the browband. It should not press tightly on to the base of the horse's ears. As the horse moves the browband should not move up and down

Throatlash — Ideally this should not be fastened on the first or last hole, so there is room for adjustment if required. It should not move excessively or press into the horse's throat when the horse is working

Noseband — This will vary in position depending on type but, for all, side straps should be clear from the horse's eyes and not rubbing the projecting cheek bones; the front strap should be clear of the bottom of the projecting cheek bones and not be so low as to restrict breathing

Bit — You should be able to fit a little finger between the sides and either side of the mouth when the bit sits straight across the tongue. The bit should be high enough in the mouth so as to slightly wrinkle the corners of the lips. It should not be so low that it dangles in the horse's mouth

Correctly fitted bridle.

You should be able fit three fingers between the withers and front of saddle (this will depend on the type of headplate and type of horse) and one finger at either side of the withers (without a rider)

The saddle must not touch the spine at the back of the gullet, and should sit level from front to back when viewed from the side, so that the rider is not tipped forwards or backwards

The front of the saddle should mirror the contours of the horse's shoulders; there should not be obvious tight spots

The saddle should look a suitable length for the horse — neither obviously too long or too short

Correctly fitted saddle.

Cleaning tack

Ideally, tack should be wiped over with a warm, damp cloth every time it is used to prevent a build-up of grease. The bit should be scrubbed clean after every use to prevent a build-up of slobber. Leather that is regularly cared for will last longer, be softer and more pliable, and is less likely to crack and split.

Prior to giving tack a full cleaning, assemble everything you will need; a bucket of warm water, sponges, saddle soap, leather balm, neatsfoot oil (or similar) and a brush. An old towel or cloth is useful and metal polish can put a shine on the buckles if you wish.

Taking the tack apart to clean it (known as strip cleaning) is the ideal time to check it over for wear and tear (see below). When strip cleaning a bridle you will need to undo all buckles and take the bridle fully apart, laying the pieces on a towel. Before you take the bridle apart remember to write down which holes the buckles are fastened on so you can put it back as it was. The bit can be soaked in hot water. When cleaning the saddle, remove the pad from the saddle to be washed or brushed off. Then remove the stirrup leathers and girth, take the stirrup irons off the leathers and wash them in warm water. You could also take the treads out of the stirrups to clean beneath them.

Items needed for tack cleaning.

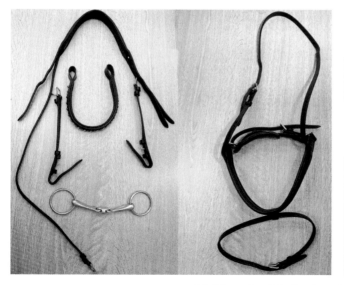
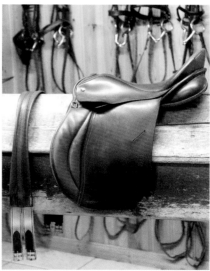

A bridle and saddle that have been taken apart in preparation for cleaning.

There are many different tack-cleaning products on the market and everyone will have their own preferred products and method. It doesn't matter which you follow so long as the grease is removed, the leather conditioned and the tack checked for safety. The basic process is as follows.

Use a hot, damp cloth or sponge to remove the grease from the leather. Be careful not to soak the leather with water or it will become dull. If the tack has not been cleaned for some time, or has been well used, you might find stubborn lumps of grease. Try loosening them by holding the hot cloth over them, then gently scraping with your fingernail. It is really important to be thorough and pay attention to the underside of the browband and noseband, and the inside of the reins where grease tends to build up. Once clean, leave the tack to dry naturally; too much heat encourages cracks.

Once dry, apply saddle soap in small circular motions with a damp sponge. The underside of the leather tends to absorb the soap better as it is rougher. Your sponge should be just wet enough to take up the soap; if it foams, the leather it is too wet and this will leave the tack feeling sticky.

All tack will benefit from an occasional application of leather balm or oil to help condition the leather and keep it supple. Balm can be rubbed in using a clean sponge or cloth, according to the manufacturer's instructions. It can add condition, waterproof the leather and make it shine. Oil also improves the leather's condition and waterproofing and restores suppleness. It is best applied with a brush (such as a clean hoof oil brush, small paintbrush or soft toothbrush) to get into the folds of leather. Apply it sparingly and allow it to soak in.

Checking tack for safety

This can easily be done while you clean it. Leather can crack and wear, particularly where it doubles over (e.g. where reins loop round the bit). If the same hole is used continuously it can weaken the leather, particularly on stirrup leathers and girth straps, which withstand a lot of pressure. Stitching needs to be checked thoroughly as it can cause safety problems if it comes

Areas where the stitching needs to be checked; stirrup leathers, girth straps and behind the billets or buckles on the bridle (most importantly on the reins and cheek pieces).

undone or rots — especially in reins and stirrup leathers. It is also a good idea to check the stitching on any keepers, noting any that are missing. Leather should also be checked in the areas where it comes into contact with leather (as with the loops in reins) for signs of wear or splitting.

A hole in a stirrup leather, showing wear.

Putting the bridle and saddle back together again

There is no set way to do this but it may be useful to remember the following points:

- Once you have the browband and the headpiece together correctly, reconstructing the rest of the bridle is relatively simple.

- Billets sit on the inside of the bridle against the horse's face.

- Buckles sit on the outside.

- Make sure the bit is not twisted and is the correct way up.

- When putting the browband on the headpiece remember that the throatlash fastens up on the left side.

- The noseband buckle also fastens on the left side.

- Cheekpieces should be on the same hole on each side. You can't put these on until the headpiece and browband are put together.

- Some nosebands sit on top of the headpiece and some below, depending on the design of the bridle. Make sure the noseband is threaded through any keepers on the headpiece.

- It is important to swap the stirrup leathers over regularly between left and right. This will prevent the same leather from being permanently on the left side (the side used for mounting) and thus stretching over time more than the one on the right-hand side.

Summary

- The horse's comfort is important when tacking up. Be gentle and pay attention to the horse's body language and facial expressions.

- If you are not sure something fits correctly ask for help and advice. Always check any tack you put on.

- The bridle should allow four fingers between the throatlash and the cheek; the bit should just wrinkle the corners of the mouth; you should be able to fit at least one finger between the noseband strap and the horse's face.

- Saddles should accommodate two or three fingers between the withers and the pommel and at least one on either side of the withers. They should sit level when viewed from the side.

- Girths are normally attached to the first and third girth straps and should be fastened gently and tightened up gradually.

- Tack should be checked for safety regularly, including stitching, holes in leather straps, and for any sign of damage.

- Clean tack frequently to prolong its life and keep it smart.

TRAINING TIPS

1. The more you handle tack the easier it becomes.

2. Every time you see a horse with tack on, pay attention and think about how everything is positioned.

3. Volunteer to tack up as much as possible; you will benefit from lots of practice with different types of tack and horses.

4. Watch your coach/yard manager when they tack up — you may pick up useful hints and tips.

5. Find out if a saddle fitter is due to visit your yard and observe them at work. Most won't mind if you ask questions at an appropriate time. It's a great way to find out what to look for.

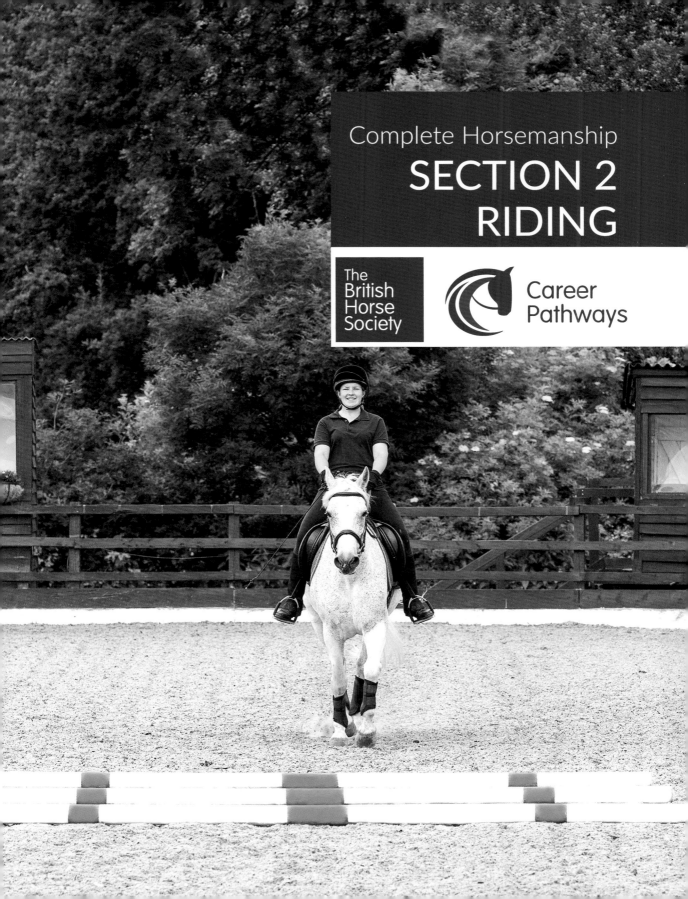

Complete Horsemanship

SECTION 2
RIDING

The British Horse Society

Career Pathways

Chapter 12

Riding a Horse on the Flat

Preparing to ride

Before leading the horse you are going to ride to the arena, take a step back to check that, so far as you can see, he has the right tack for what you are going to do. Someone else may have tacked up and if a martingale or pair of boots have been forgotten, it's best to find out now. This is also a good time to check the tack for safety. While the yard manager will also check tack regularly, it's up to you to speak up if you see any worn/split leather or loose stitching.

Check that the numnah has been pulled up into the pommel and is not pressing on the withers. If it has straps, these should be properly attached so that the numnah will not slip during your ride. Finally, check you have everything you need; whip, gloves, etc. Double-check that the saddle is still in the correct position and the girth is tight enough to keep it from sliding back while leading. The stirrups should be left run up, so they do not get caught on the stable door or arena gate, or bang against the horse as he walks. Also, check that stirrups seem to be the correct size for your feet — those that are evidently too big or too small can be hazardous.

Then make your way to the arena, leading the horse much as you would in a headcollar; take the reins over the head and hold them as you would the lead rope. However, if the horse is wearing a martingale, leave the reins on the neck, otherwise the martingale straps can become tangled with the reins and impede your control. It is best to hold both reins in the right hand under the horse's chin, to have maximum control. If you have a whip, keep it in your left hand away from the horse.

Take the reins over the horse's head and hold them in the same way as a lead rope.

Leave the reins on the horse's neck and use your right hand to hold both reins just behind the horse's chin.

Preparation before mounting

If there are other people and horses in the arena you should always knock and ask if you may enter, to alert them that you are there and give them time to move away from the gate. Always make sure that any arena gates or doors are closed behind you (if a horse gets loose this will contain him within a safe area).

Lead the horse to the middle of the arena, away from the gate or door and from other horses already using the space. If there is a seating area, it is best to position the horse towards this so he can see what is going on, and any noise from people moving around will be less likely to startle him. If you are in a group, be aware of where the others are. It is best to face in the same direction and to space yourselves out well, as you need to be able to move around your horse easily without the risk of being kicked or squashed. You should aim to leave at least one horse's length — around 2m between each horse.

Once you have found a safe place to stand, prepare your tack for mounting, while keeping control of the horse so that he does not walk off or get too close to another horse. If you need both hands free, for example to tighten the girth, you loop your arm through the reins to avoid dropping them. Be careful not to pull the reins accidentally as you move around; the horse may think you want him to turn with you. If you are carrying a whip, take care not to touch or startle him accidentally with it. You may find it easier to tuck the whip out of the way under your arm when you need your hands free. Make sure everything is comfortable for the horse and that all straps are secured, tucked into keepers and not flapping. Check that the saddle is still in the correct position and has not slipped back on the way to the arena. The girth will need to be tightened firmly enough so that the saddle will not slip when you mount, yet still allowing you to fit your hand flat between the girth and the horse.

The stirrups can then be run down. It is a good idea to check that the stirrup leathers are roughly the right length for you before getting on; it is easier to adjust them from the ground, especially if the leathers are a bit stiff. If the horse were to move off suddenly when you mount, you will stay better in balance and be safer if your stirrup leathers are approximately the right length.

Check that the stirrup leathers are roughly the correct length for you before mounting.

You can estimate an approximate length by holding your fist to the stirrup bar and stretching the leather down your arm with the stirrup iron towards your armpit. With a straight arm, the stirrup iron should reach into your armpit if the stirrup leather is roughly the right length. The ratio of arm to leg length will vary from person to person, so practise this until you know what measurement works for you. Those with longer legs and shorter arms may need some slack in the leather when the iron hits the armpit.

It is best not to rely on the numbering on stirrup leathers, as the leather may have stretched more on one side than the other. So, to check that the stirrups are level you will need to stand in front of the horse to compare both stirrups simultaneously. Make sure the saddle is sitting level and the horse is not resting a hind leg; such things can make the stirrups look uneven even if they are not. But be aware of what the horse is doing as you check the stirrups; you are vulnerable if he suddenly moves forward.

Mounting

Where possible, it is best to use a mounting block to get on, as this puts less pressure on the horse's back and the saddle. However, this may not always be possible, so once you are comfortable with mounting from a block it is a good idea to practise mounting from the ground so that you can do either if needed.

When leading the horse to the mounting block, leave the reins on the horse's neck and hold both together behind his chin. Walk towards the mounting block in a straight line, parallel to it. This saves you having to manoeuvre the horse into position to mount; the more you move a horse around the less likely he is to stand quietly. For ease of mounting and safety you ideally want the horse to halt with the nearside stirrup level to the centre of the mounting block, with enough room between him and the block to allow you to mount easily and safely. If the horse is too close to the block, there is a risk that he will knock his legs into it as he moves away, which could frighten him into rushing forwards. Equally, too big a gap could force you to throw yourself at the horse in an attempt to get on. A gap between block and horse of around 30–40cm (1ft–1ft 4in) is ideal. The horse should stand squarely if possible, not resting a hind leg, so that he is able to keep his balance when you mount. Position the horse correctly before stepping on to the mounting block, as it is much harder to move him once you are up there.

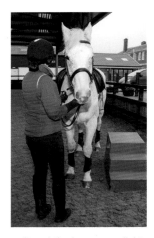

Stand the horse parallel to the mounting block with sufficient space between him and the block before starting to mount.

Once the horse is in position, step on to the mounting block, taking care to keep control so that he does not move off or try to turn around before you are ready. Gather up the reins into your left hand and tuck the excess rein down the offside of the horse's neck out of the way. Your whip should also be placed down the side of the horse's neck. The whip can be placed on the near- or offside, but if someone is helping you mount, carry it on the opposite side to them to avoid accidentally hitting them.

Place your left foot in the stirrup so that it sits on the widest part of the foot. You can use your right hand to hold the stirrup still if necessary. Putting your foot too far through the stirrup is dangerous; not far enough through and your toe may slip out. The stirrup leather should lie flat against the saddle and horse. Take care to turn your toe out slightly so it does not dig into the horse's side and cause discomfort. Your right hand can then be placed on the far side of the pommel, to help with balance as you mount. You should not hold the back of the saddle with your right hand, as this may cause you to pull the saddle towards you, which can affect the positioning of the saddle.

Push up from the mounting block using your right leg and, with your body weight centred over the saddle, use the 'spring' and momentum to swing your right leg up and over the horse's back. Take care not to touch him with your leg or foot. Gently bring your right leg down the far side and into position, lightly lowering your seat into the saddle to avoid thumping your weight down and hurting the horse. Place your right foot into the stirrup as you do so — imagine sitting down on a fragile chair that may break if you land too hard. Take the reins in each hand, then move away from the mounting block in a straight line so that the horse does not catch a leg on the block.

Try to position the horse and mount without taking too long. Even the quietest, sweetest-natured horse can get distracted and wander off if you do. Once safely on board, return to your space in the middle of the arena so you can safely recheck the girth and adjust your stirrups further as required.

i. Hold the reins in the left hand and place the left foot into the stirrup, taking care not to dig the toe into the horse.

ii. Reins should be short enough to keep the horse under control with your hands positioned to help you balance while you mount.

iii. Push up from the mounting block and centre your weight over the saddle.

iv Swing your right leg over the horse's back, taking care not to kick him, and sit lightly into the saddle.

Adjusting the girth once mounted

It is a good idea to check your girth once mounted as the added weight in the saddle will quite often mean the girth becomes looser. You should also check the girth again once you have warmed up the horse and the saddle settles into place. To check if it's tight enough, place both reins and whip into the opposite hand of the side you are going to check, before leaning forward and sliding your hand between the horse's side and the girth, just behind the elbow. You should be able to fit a flat hand comfortably under the girth; if you can fit more than that you will need to tighten it. You should also be careful not to over-tighten the girth, as this can restrict the horse from expanding his lungs fully as he breathes.

A flat hand should fit under the girth.

To alter the girth, swing your leg quietly forward in front of the saddle, keeping the foot in the stirrup and taking care not to kick the horse's shoulder. Lift the saddle flap and gently adjust the girth, using your finger to guide the pin into the hole. Be careful not to tighten the girth too quickly as the horse may not like the sudden tightening effect.

The buckle guard needs to be pulled back down over the buckles afterwards so that it can do its job of protecting the leather of the saddle flap. The saddle flap can then be placed back down before putting your leg gently back in position and taking the reins back into two hands ready to ride on.

If you need to check or adjust your girth at any point during a ridden session you first need to find a suitable place to halt that isn't too close to the wall or fence and isn't in the way of other riders. The middle of the school is usually a good place.

Make sure you tighten the girth gently.

The buckle guard protects the saddle flap from the buckles, so needs to be put back in place after the girth has been adjusted.

Adjusting the stirrups

Once you have mounted you may need to adjust the stirrup leathers so that the stirrups are at a comfortable length. (You will also need to adjust them when moving from flatwork to working over poles or jumping.) It is important to remain safe and in control as you do so. Keep both feet in the stirrups in case the horse moves off suddenly. Have your reins short enough to keep control, then place them and the whip into the opposite hand to the side of the stirrup you are altering.

To alter the length of the stirrup leathers you will need to do the following:

1. Remove the end of the leather from the keeper.

2. Take hold of the buckle and pull it away from the stirrup bar, then undo the buckle.

3. To shorten the leather, lighten the foot slightly to allow the pin to move upwards.

4. To lengthen the leather, push a little more weight into the foot to move the pin down.

5. Use your finger to guide the pin into the correct hole, making sure you remember which hole you started on.

6. Move the buckle back up to the stirrup bar by holding on to the top of the stirrup leather and pressing down on the iron with your foot; this act like a lever and slides the buckle back to the top.

7. Replace the end of the leather into the keeper, making sure it is lying flat against the saddle.

8. Repeat on the opposite side to make sure the length of the stirrup leathers remains level.

Keeping both feet in the stirrups, remove the end of the leather from the keeper before pulling the buckle down.

Dismounting

When you have finished riding, find a suitable place to dismount, with enough space to do so safely without impeding anyone still riding. The middle of the arena is the safest place. If a group of riders are all dismounting at the same time, they should line up with enough space between each horse. Once halted, keep the reins short enough to keep control and put both reins and your whip into your left hand. The right hand can be placed on the front of the saddle to help. Remove both feet from the stirrups, lean forward slightly and, at the same time, swing your right leg backwards and over the back of the horse and saddle, taking care not to touch the horse with your foot or leg. Once both legs are on the left side of the horse, drop down and land lightly on the floor. Bend your knees as you land to absorb the impact and help you keep your balance. The stirrups can then be run up and the girth slackened a hole before leading the horse back to the yard. If someone else is dismounting near you, it is best not to lead your horse away until they have done so, as their horse is likely to want to follow yours.

With both feet out of the stirrups, lean forward slightly before swinging your right leg backwards with enough energy to allow some lift out of the saddle.

Take care to swing your leg clear of the horse's quarters, then bend your knees as you land.

Rider's position

Developing the correct riding position is something that you will spend a lot of time working towards. The aim is that a rider should be sitting over the centre of the horse, where he can carry the weight of the rider and balance himself more easily. To achieve the correct position and be in balance you should start by sitting square in the centre of the saddle with your weight evenly carried over both seat bones. You should sit up straight without any tension and support your own weight, which will enable you to move in harmony with the horse.

When you are sitting in the correct position you should be able to draw an imaginary perpendicular line from ear, shoulder, hip to heel.

Head

Your head and neck should be square on your shoulders and not tilted to either side, as your head is heavy and this will have an effect on the rest of your body. Make sure you are looking in the direction you are travelling. If you need to check your diagonal or canter lead (see later this chapter) make sure you glance down rather than dropping your whole head down.

Rider looking up and ahead.

Shoulders

Your shoulders should be level and relaxed, not forced down and back. They need to be supple so you can follow the movement of the horse's head.

Arms

Your upper arms should be relaxed and carried close to the upper body, with a bend in your elbows. Your elbows should not be stretched in front of you or clamped to your sides. They should be supple to allow you to feel what is happening at the end of the reins. When viewed from the side there should be a straight line running from the elbow to the rein and to the horse's mouth.

Straight line from rider's elbow, down the rein to the horse's mouth.

Hands

The hands should be carried on either side of the horse's neck, positioned so that your thumbs are on top and your knuckles are facing outwards. Each rein should be tucked between your little finger and your ring finger and come out over the top of the hand. Your fingers should be closed around the reins without being clenched, to allow you to feel what the horse is doing.

The correct way to hold the reins.

Back

Your back should be straight, allowing for the natural curve of your spine.

Waist and hips

These should be straight and not collapsed either to one side, forwards or backwards.

Legs

Your legs should hang around the horse's sides with the natural weight dropped down to your feet. The knees should be relaxed to allow the legs to sit around the horse's sides and the heels to sit vertically under your hips.

Feet

Your feet should be positioned so that the stirrup irons sit across the widest part, with your toes facing forwards and your heels sitting slightly lower than your toes.

When viewed from the back there should be a straight line down the centre of the rider's head, down the middle of their back, through the middle of the saddle and the horse's spine. The shoulders should be level and the head carried straight.

When viewed from behind, the rider should be sitting straight. This rider is looking slightly to the right but her shoulders and back are straight.

The horse's gaits

Understanding the sequence and beats of the footfalls in each gait allows you to understand how the horse is moving his body and how this might affect you as a rider. Although the sequence of footfalls is the same for each horse, all horses will move in slightly different ways owing to many factors, such as their conformation or level of training. Therefore, every horse will give you a different feel and teach you something new.

Walk

The walk is a four-beat gait. To maintain the correct position you have to allow your lower back and hips to move in harmony with the horse's movement.

In walk the horse will nod his head in time with the forelegs being placed forwards on the ground. To keep a consistent rein contact you have to ensure that your elbows are supple enough to allow the horse to move your arms gently forward and back with the nodding of the head.

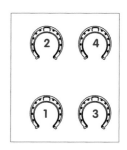

Footfalls in walk.

Trot

Trot is a two-beat gait in which the horse moves his legs in diagonal pairs, with a moment of suspension between each pair. The trot has more spring than the walk and you have the choice of sitting or rising to it. Most trot work will be carried out rising until you get to the higher levels of dressage.

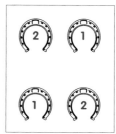

Footfalls in trot.

In rising trot you will sit for one beat and rise for the other. To allow for the horse moving underneath you, you will need to bring your upper body very slightly forwards from the hips and allow your hips to swing up and forwards just enough to clear the saddle, using the movement produced by the horse. The 'sit' into the saddle should be controlled so that you land lightly without allowing your weight and upper body to fall back.

Trot diagonals

To stay in balance with the horse in rising trot, you should be rising when the horse's outside shoulder moves forward and sitting as it comes back. To check which diagonal you are on, glance down at the outside shoulder and watch for it moving forward and back. If you find you are sitting as it swings forward, you will need to change your diagonal by sitting for an extra beat before rising again. As you become more practised you will be able to feel whether you are on the correct diagonal. Each time you change the rein aim to change your diagonal before you turn on to the new rein so you are able to help the horse stay in balance.

You should rise as the horse's outside[1] foreleg moves forward and sit as the inside foreleg moves forward.

1 Inside and outside — these terms refer to the inside and outside of the curve of the horse, which is not necessarily the same as the inside and outside of the arena.

In sitting trot you stay in contact with the saddle by sitting softly in the saddle, keeping your body upright and absorbing the movement of the horse's back through your seat, lower back and thighs.

Canter

Canter is a three-beat gait with a moment of suspension after the third beat. The horse's back lifts with each stride and you need to absorb this movement through your lower back, seat and legs, keeping your legs 'long', and not 'rowing' with the upper body. Your upper body should stay upright and your elbows soft and flexible, moving in harmony with the horse and keeping the rein contact consistent.

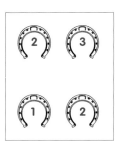

Footfalls in canter.

Canter leads

In canter, one foreleg reaches further forward than the other and this is referred to as the leading leg. To help the horse stay in balance the leading leg should be the left fore on the left rein and the right fore on the right rein. You will learn to feel whether the horse is on the correct lead but, until you are confident, glance down at the shoulders and watch for which one is coming further forward. When the horse is on the correct lead, the movement should feel smooth and balanced. If the horse is on the wrong lead it will feel lumpy and unbalanced and the horse may struggle to stay in canter. If you do pick up the wrong lead (see Aids), return to trot and rebalance the horse. Wait for the next corner of the arena and reapply the aids, making sure you are asking clearly.

The rider is in balance with the horse in canter.

Control of the horse

The aids

The aids are the signals a rider uses to communicate with the horse, such as the rider's legs, seat, hands and voice. They also include the use of the whip or spurs. The legs, seat and hands are used together to influence the horse.

The legs should remain in a soft contact with the horse's sides rather than be used continuously. To ask the horse to move forwards, the rider should increase the pressure of the legs around the horse's sides and then relax the legs again when the horse has responded. It may be necessary to repeat this if the desired response is not achieved.

When first learning, the rider should concentrate on keeping their seat supple enough to go with the movement of the horse's back and not interfere with his rhythm.

The reins are used to help control the speed and direction of the horse. They should be used gently, with a gradual increase in pressure to gain a response, and should not be used as a balancing aid by the rider.

A short whip can be used to back up the rider's leg aids, if the horse is not responding. The whip is carried in the inside hand and rests across the rider's thigh just above the knee. If you need to use the whip, place the reins into the opposite hand and tap the horse behind your inside leg then retake the reins in both hands.

The whip should be swapped into the opposite hand when a change of rein is made. Try to pick a time that will not interrupt the flow of a change of rein. Sometimes it may be better to wait until the change of rein is complete and the new rein established before swapping the whip over.

To swap the whip over from left to right. Place both reins in your left hand. Use your right hand to pull the whip through the top of your left hand. Lift the whip over the horse's neck. Place the whip over your right thigh and retake your reins.

Turning

The aids for turning, whether to make a corner or a circle, are the same:

- Check your position.

- Look in the direction in which you want to turn.

- Use the inside rein gently to guide the horse around the turn.

- Move your outside leg slightly behind the girth to encourage the horse to bring his quarters around the turn, and apply pressure with your leg.

- Apply your inside leg by the girth to encourage the horse to bend around the turn and to keep the forward impulse.

- Keep a contact down your outside rein to control the horse's outside shoulder.

- Your hips and shoulders should follow the position of the horse around the turn.

Transitions

Moving the horse from one gait to another, which includes riding into/out of halt, is called riding a transition. A good transition should be ridden smoothly and appear seamless.

Before riding any transition, always do a quick check of your own position.

Upward transitions

- Maintain a feel through the reins.

- Close your legs around the horse's sides and increase the pressure through your calves to ask him to move forward into the required new gait.

- Relax the pressure when the horse responds.

- Soften your elbows as he starts to move forward and allow your arms to move with the head and neck.

- Make sure the new gait is active.

Canter transitions

- To encourage the horse to pick up the correct lead, ask for canter in a corner, or on a curved line.

- Take sitting trot a few strides before you ask for canter.

- Keep your inside leg on the girth and position your outside leg slightly further back. Ask the horse to move forwards into canter by increasing the pressure through your calves.

Downward transitions

- Check your position.

- Sit up and think about 'slowing' the movement with your seat.

- Gradually and gently increase the pressure down the reins until the horse changes his gait.

- Have your legs gently against the horse's sides and ride forward in the new gait.

If response is lacking

If you feel the horse is not responding to your aids:

- Check that you have applied the aids correctly.

- You may need to apply the aids more than once, but it is better to repeat the aids rather than give one long continuous aid.

- Make sure the horse is working actively before asking for a transition. A horse who is walking slowly is unlikely to spring into trot.

Warming up and cooling down

So that the horse may carry out his work efficiently and with minimal strain or risk of injury, it is advisable to warm him up at the start of a work session just as a human athlete would. Warming up the horse not only allows him to prepare mentally and physically for work; it increases the blood flow around the body and allows his muscles, tendons and ligaments to warm up, increasing the range of movement and therefore reducing the risk of injury. Each horse is an individual and their warm-up requirements will differ, but an active walk on a long rein is a good place to start; it also gives the rider a chance to warm up before progressing to trot and canter. The work should be carried out on both reins to aid the horse's suppleness. If it is cold, or the horse is clipped out, you may want to put an exercise sheet over his back to keep the muscles warm when first starting off.

Cooling off a horse at the end of a session is just as important as warming up at the start of a session. It allows the horse's heart and respiration rates to return to normal and the muscles to cool down gradually, reducing the risk of stiffness the next day. The horse should be walked until his breathing has returned to normal before being taken back to his stable to be untacked and washed or brushed off as required. If it is cold, or the horse is very sweaty, putting an exercise sheet over his back will stop him getting a chill.

Cooling down.

Riding school figures and over poles

Basic principles

When riding in an arena you will ride various movements and shapes, including changes of direction. It is important to ride in both directions to avoid the horse becoming crooked or 'one-sided'. The shapes you ride are called school figures. Dressage tests are simply several school figures linked together. You will need to think about the accuracy of the school figures when you are riding them to ensure they are the correct shape to help the horse bend evenly.

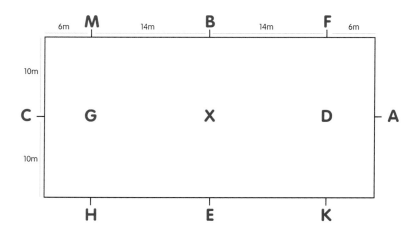

A standard dressage arena measuring 20m wide and 40m long.

In order to fully understand school figures and how to ride them, you first need to know the size of an arena and the letters that are placed around it. There are two sizes of dressage arena: 20m wide by 40m long is a standard arena, and 20m wide by 60m is known as a long arena. The size of arenas at different yards can vary massively, depending on the space available. It is a good idea to know the size of the arena you are riding in to be able to ride accurate school figures.

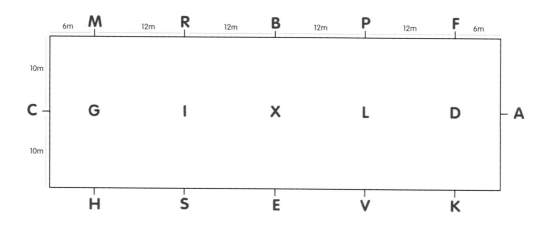

An international-sized dressage arena measuring 20m wide and 60m long.

20m circle

A 20m circle measures 20m across the diameter. These circles are usually ridden at either end of the arena (at A or C) or in the centre of the arena (at E or B). It may be easier to begin riding

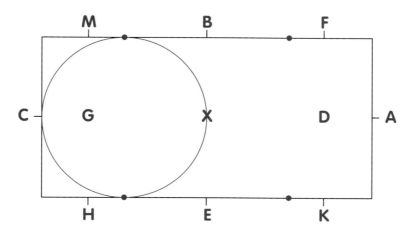

*When riding a 20m circle at C in a 20 x 40m arena,
the circle should touch the arena at both sides and come halfway down the arena through X.*

circles in walk initially to give you more time to plan where you are going to ride, and move on to trot once you are more confident. Riding a true circle is not as easy to master as you may think.

The letter C in the illustration indicates where the circle should start and finish. When thinking about riding a circle, it is a good idea to split it into four quarters with four 'marker' points and ride from one point to the next on a curved line, making sure you do not ride a straight line at any point on the circle. Your shoulders should always face the direction you are moving. In this case, they should be turned slightly to the inside of the circle, and you should be looking up and around the circle to the next point.

If you are riding the circle in the centre of the arena (at E or B) the same principles apply, but you will not have three sides of the arena to help you. Once you are confident riding a 20m circle using the arena and letters to guide you, you can progress to riding an accurate 20m circle anywhere, although this is a skill that requires a lot of practice.

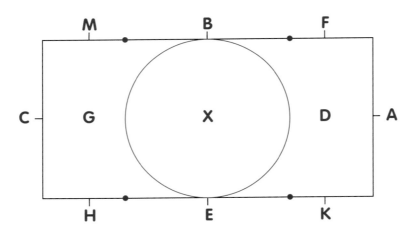

When riding a 20m circle at E in a 20 x 40m arena, the circle should touch the arena at E and B and cross the centre line 10m either side of X.

The most common mistake when riding a circle is not making it circle-shaped, and making the circle either too big or too small. Looking where you want to ride will help, but you will also need to use both legs to keep the horse moving in the direction you want. If the circle is too small or the horse tries to cut the corner, you will need to use more inside leg to push him out while still keeping him looking in the direction he is going. If the circle is too big or the horse is falling towards the outside, you will need to use more outside leg to support him and prevent this.

Changes of rein

A change of rein is simply a way of changing the direction in which you ride around the arena, and often makes use of the letters around the arena as start and finish markers.

Long diagonal

This is a change of rein by riding from a letter near one corner of the arena (known as the 'quarter marker' to the letter near the diagonally opposite corner, passing through X in the centre of the arena, for example, MXK. The aim is to ride through the corner between the short and long side of the arena before making a turn at the letter M, then travel across the diagonal through X to be back on the track at K. Aim to reach the track just before K, so the horse is on the track at K and you are able to ride into the next corner.

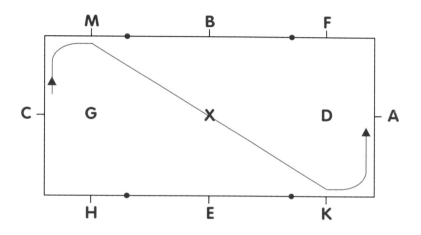

Riding the turns at the quarter markers well will help to make the change of rein more accurate.

Short diagonal

This change of rein is very similar to the long diagonal, but does not use the marker letters near both ends of the arena. A short diagonal will take you either from a quarter marker to E or B or vice versa, for example M to E or B to K. You need to ride this using the same principles as the long diagonal, but the turns at either end will be slightly more acute, meaning you may need slightly more leg aids to move the horse around the turns.

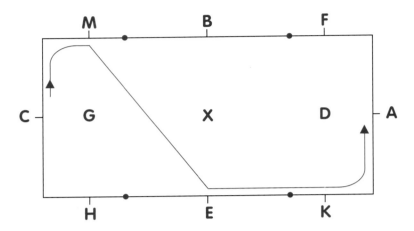

Look ahead to help you keep straight across the diagonal.

Centre line

This is a change of rein down the centre line and can be ridden in either direction (A to C or C to A). Every dressage test starts and finishes with riding down the centre line from A, towards C where the judge sits. The turn on to the centre line should be a smooth curve rather than an abrupt turn, and for this you need to look ahead, keeping your eyes on where you want to go so that you can judge where to turn. The turn off the centre line also needs to be an arc, looking ahead around the bend to judge when to leave the centre line. To help keep yourself straight as you ride down the centre line, it is a good idea to keep your eyes on a fixed point above C and use both legs to ride forwards and straight. Whether you are turning on to the centre line or riding straight down it, your body and head need to be facing the way you are moving, and the horse should follow that line through his body while looking in the direction in which he is travelling.

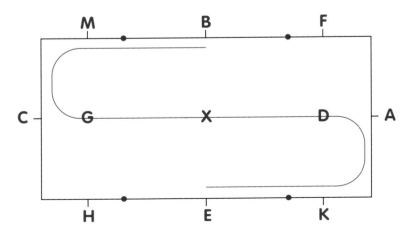

Smooth curves on and off the centre line, with a straight line between.

E to B

This is a similar change of rein as along the centre line, but riding between E and B (in either direction) means across the arena, so there is a shorter straight line between the turns. The turns will still be smooth arcs, and you can help achieve this by looking ahead to where you are aiming to go.

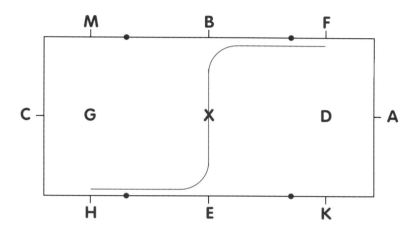

Keeping your eyes on where you want to ride will help to get you there.

Two 20m half-circles

This is an S-shape movement down the length of the (20 x 40m) arena, using similar techniques as for a full 20m circle. This can be ridden from either the A or the C end, finishing

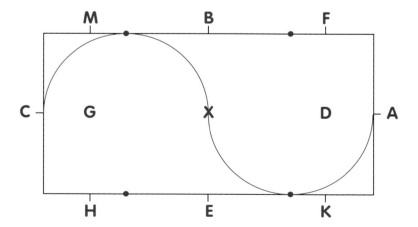

When riding half-circles, to be as accurate as possible,
you need to ride as you would for a full 20m circle at either end of the arena, but only ride half of each circle.

at the opposite end in order to change direction. For example, starting at A on the right rein, you start to ride a 20m circle but, when you reach X, you then start a 20m circle on the left rein into the opposite end of the arena, towards C.

The first half of the circle (in this case on the right rein) will need to be ridden with slight right bend so that the horse's body is following the curve of the circle. When approaching X you need to think about changing on to the other circle, which will mean a change of rein (and therefore the direction that you and the horse are facing). When you cross X, you need to move on to the left rein circle, looking ahead to where you are going and asking the horse to do the same using your legs.

Two 10m half-circles

This is a similar movement to the above, but uses a smaller area by working across the width of the arena. This can be done in either direction, and is generally done from E to B or B to E. Until you are comfortable with the shaping, it is a good idea to do this in walk to give you more time to plan where you are riding, before progressing to the same movement in trot. A common mistake is to ride the half-circles too small (too shallow), so it is a good idea to practise riding a full 10m circle at E until you are comfortable with the size before then swapping on to the 10m circle to B when you reach X. It is important that, when riding through X, you should be on the centre line facing A or C, before swapping to the opposite half-circle.

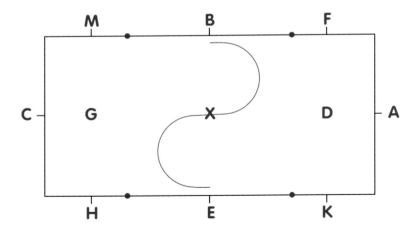

Looking ahead to the next point on your half-circle helps you achieve accuracy in terms of direction and size.

Half-circle returns

This is a school figure commonly used in dressage tests to change the direction by combining two movements. It is a half-circle starting on the track, followed by a straight line on a diagonal to bring you back to the track on the same side of the arena as you started from, but facing the opposite direction.

The size of the half-circle can vary, as will the point you need to return to the track, but the same principles apply. When riding a 10m half-circle at K, this will not quite touch the end of the arena (it will be 1m short) and it will end at D. To then return to the track, you will need to ride from D to H, aiming to touch the track just before H so that you are straight on the track by H. If the half-circle is 15m, you will need to start the circle earlier than the corner letter in order to fit it in, so in a dressage test you would be asked to start your half-circle between E and K. To make this as easy to ride as possible, starting the 15m half-circle 1.5m short of K will enable you then to just touch the end of the arena, bringing you around to a point halfway between the centre line and the far side of the arena (i.e. on to the three-quarter line). If you are asked to return to the track between two letters, it is a good idea to aim to touch the track in plenty of time so that you do not overshoot the second letter. This will also give you plenty of time to prepare for riding the corner.

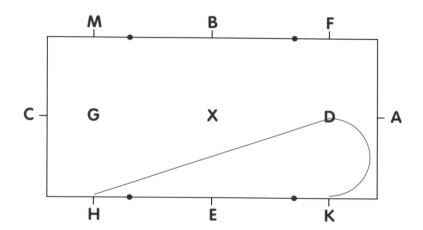

Riding a 10m half-circle at K, returning to the track at H.
Splitting the movement into a half-circle and a straight line will help to maintain accuracy.

Figures that maintain the same rein

Figure-of-eight

The figure-of-eight is a movement that makes the shape of an 8 in the arena. Most commonly in a 20 x 40m arena it comprises two 20m circles, one at A and one at C, linked together at X. Typically you would ride two 20m half-circles starting from A or C (see description of these figures above), followed immediately by two more 20m half-circles, which would bring you back to the starting letter facing the same direction you started.

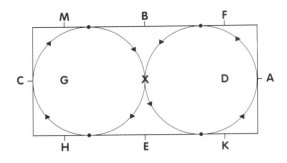

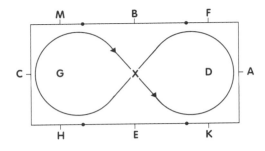

A figure-of-eight ridden by linking two 20m circles through X, showing two changes of rein.

A figure-of-eight using straight lines across the diagonals.

A figure-of-eight can also be ridden across two consecutive diagonals with a half-circle past A or C in between, although this is less common.

Three-loop serpentine

A three-loop serpentine is a snake-like shape down the arena with three equal-sized loops, starting at either A or C and finishing at the opposite end. Each loop needs to be a third of the arena length, so before starting the serpentine you should visualise splitting the arena into three. Each curve touches the side of the arena, after which you ride across the arena in a straight line, parallel with the arena's short sides, and then curve the opposite way. Keep looking ahead as you ride the serpentine so that you get to where you want to be, turning your head to look around the curves and keeping your eyes on a fixed point to keep you straight as you ride the lines between them.

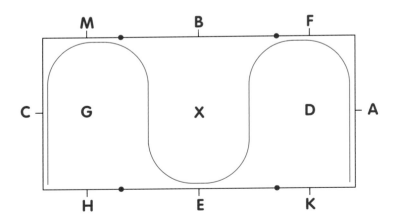

The three-loop serpentine needs to touch the sides of the arena, have three equal loops, and straight lines when crossing the centre line.

Shallow loop (5m)

This school figure is ridden using the corners and the long side of the arena. For example, ride into the corner then, at K, ride to a point 5m in from the track halfway between E and X, before riding back to the track just short of H, then finish by riding into the corner. This needs to be ridden as a smooth curve rather than straight lines, with your body and the horse facing the direction in which you are travelling.

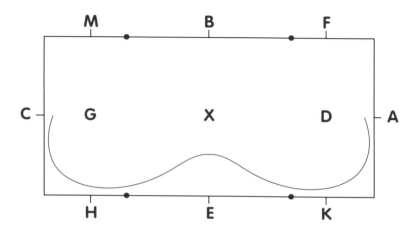

When riding a shallow loop, look to the next point in the curve so that the size and shape of the loop are accurate.

Planning and looking ahead

The key to riding any school figure well is to plan where you are going before you start and to keep looking in that direction.

Riding over poles

When riding exercises involving poles, ride them using the same principles regardless of the position and number of poles in a line.

Before approaching the pole, ensure that the trot is sufficiently energetic for the whole exercise. If you approach a line of poles lacking energy in the trot, the horse will run out of energy and may not maintain the desired striding between each pole.

It is also easier to maintain your own balance if the horse is moving in a consistent trot throughout.

Once you have a good enough trot, the exercise needs to be split up into sections. For the approach, look for a line to ride straight over the middle of the poles. Ride a turn large enough for the horse to be able to keep the same quality of trot and maintain his balance on the approach. The approach line to the poles needs to be a straight line towards the centre of the poles, and beyond it, before making a smooth, balanced turn when you reach the other end of the arena. When riding over poles, be ready to emphasise rising trot allowing your shoulder and hands to move forward.

Throughout your exercise it is important to maintain the quality of trot and avoid speeding up or slowing down. This will be made easier by keeping your own balance.

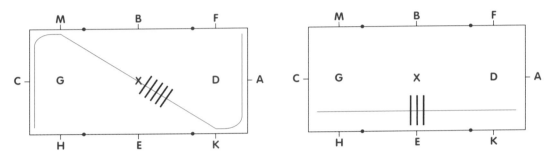

Regardless of where the poles are, ride a smooth turn on to a straight line that can be maintained through the approach, the poles and the get-away.

Riding in company

When riding in a group or 'ride' it is important to keep yourself, your horse and others safe, by keeping a minimum of one horse's length between each horse in any direction. If you are following another rider, be careful not to get too close or you risk being kicked or crashing into the horse in front if that horse were to stop suddenly. If passing another horse, for example when moving to the front of the ride, make sure you leave enough space to avoid being kicked. Some horses can be nervous about other horses passing them and might try to stop or duck away from the passing horse, or possibly even react by speeding up or kicking out.

You should keep at least one horse's distance between each horse.

A bigger gap will help them feel more comfortable. When riding around the edge of the arena on the outside track it is equally important to leave enough space between yourself and the wall/fence so neither you nor the horse ends up touching the wall/fence, which might scare him or cause an injury. When maintaining suitable distances between each horse, it is essential to be aware of other riders in the group. If you are at the front of the ride, be aware of riders behind you so you don't leave them behind. If you are the lead rider, you should adjust the speed as necessary.

If the lead rider is not moving forwards enough, it will be hard for other riders to prevent the gaps between horses becoming too small; again, the lead rider should adjust their own speed to match the others. It is the responsibility of each rider to ensure they maintain the gap between themselves and the horse in front. If you are getting left behind, you may need to turn across the school, missing out the end of the arena or the corner to catch up with the others, and then ride more forward to prevent it happening again. If you get too close, ride deeper into the corners to create more space.

You will need to learn to alter the horse's speed or direction when in a group, so you are able, for example, to move your horse away from the others in the group and circle round to take up the rear of the ride. Some horses may not be willing to do this, as they would rather follow the horse in front, so you may need to use stronger aids. The horse may also want to slow down when moving away from the others and speed up when moving back towards them, so it is important to control him in order to maintain a consistent speed.

If you need to stop for any reason (e.g. to adjust your girth or stirrup leathers, or to take a rest) find a suitable place that will not affect the others in the group. This is normally on the centre line facing the side of the arena. If more than one horse needs to stop, or if the whole group needs to, this can done by lining up on the centre line with enough space between horses (at least one horse's length) to avoid being kicked or squashed, as you would at the end of the ride before you prepare to dismount.

Leave enough space between each horse to avoid getting kicked or squashed.

Riding 'independently'

When riding at the same time as others in the arena, you will not always be in a single ride. When riding independently it is even more important to be aware of other riders and what they are doing, to avoid crashes or leaving too little space between you. This is made easier by always looking up and ahead so you can try to anticipate what other riders are doing and adapt your direction if necessary.

There are various rules that riders should follow when riding independently, which help them to work around each other safely:

- When passing a rider in opposite directions, pass left hand to left hand, with enough space between to avoid any confusion or collisions.

- If you are walking and others are riding at a faster gait, you should take the inner track (approximately 3m in from the outer track) to allow others to work around you.

- Give way to horses moving in a faster gait. This may mean halting or turning across the arena (if another horse is circling in trot, for example). By looking ahead and anticipating what other riders are doing, you may be able to adapt your own exercise to enable you to give way to another rider who is also in the middle of an exercise, e.g. by altering the size of your circle. If you need or wish to halt, do this away from the track, usually on the centre line. However, if someone is working on a 20m circle at A, it is best not to halt at X. If working in a small arena, it may be helpful if everyone rides on the same rein, and changes rein at the same time.

The key things to remember are always to look ahead and be courteous to other riders. If in any doubt, it is better to slow down or stop rather than risk a crash. Being able to ride independently without crashing is a skill that requires a lot of practice. There may be times when you accidentally get too close to another rider, or you almost crash into them (we all make mistakes at some point). The important thing is to learn from these incidents and react differently the next time. If you have a near-miss and you are not sure whether it was your fault, you could ask someone more senior about the situation. It is not about blaming someone, but about using the opportunity to learn and improve your riding.

Exercises to improve balance and suppleness

Any horse you ride will be most comfortable and perform to his best when you are sitting in balance and going with the horse's movement. Generally, balance is achieved by sitting in a correct position, but this can only be maintained if you are supple and strong enough to hold a position and able to move with the horse. Achieving this is easier said than done; we all have stiffness in different areas and tension often creeps in when we are trying to achieve something, which can work against us when we are riding. So, improving balance and suppleness will take work. Certain exercises can help. Working without stirrups develops suppleness through your lower back and hips but will also help to stretch your leg down and back, so it is naturally positioned more underneath you, which helps you to balance better. Working in light seat focuses on your ability to maintain balance in preparation for jumping and strengthens the muscles you will use when jumping. Already, at some point, you will have felt sore after riding when your muscles have been stretched. However, it is worth persevering and the more you do, the stronger and more supple you will become, which will improve your riding ability and also keep you safer in the saddle.

Work without stirrups

Before doing any work without stirrups you will need to cross your stirrups over, out of the way of your legs, and make sure they are secure.

Once you have taken your foot out of the stirrup, pull the stirrup buckle away from the bar on the saddle; this allows the leathers to cross over but remain flatter so they are less uncomfortable against your leg. When crossing the stirrups over the horse's neck, the stirrups should lie flat against his shoulders.

Work without stirrups will help your balance and suppleness through your hips and lower back. Try to relax as a much as you can, moving with the horse rather than gripping with your legs. If you grip, you might find that you bounce more. It is also much more comfortable for the horse when you relax and begin to move with him. The best way to learn to ride without stirrups is by having a lunge lesson, so you don't have to worry about controlling the horse and can concentrate on learning how to sit to him.

Simply riding without your stirrups in walk can help your position and softness. Start by letting your legs hang long and relaxed. Make sure you are sitting up tall and that the horse is walking actively. Don't make yourself move; just allow the horse to move you through the lower back and hips.

Unfortunately, trotting without stirrups might not be so easy. But the same principles apply: it's a good idea to start by holding the front of the saddle with one hand. Pulling up on the front of the saddle will keep you secure, and you should gradually be able to lighten your grip until you can let go. You should feel your core muscles working, particularly so in the trot, to keep you secure in the saddle. Your main core muscles are situated in your belly and middle and lower back. It is best to start by trotting for a few strides and then walking again, concentrating on using your core muscles but staying soft through the remainder of your body without gripping up. Over time you will be able to build up to trotting for longer periods. The aim is to be able to sit to the trot, maintaining your position, with an independent, steady rein contact.

A lunge lesson is the best way to learn how to ride without stirrups, as you can concentrate on learning how to sit to the trot without having to worry about controlling the horse.

Finding your core

If you are not sure where your core muscles are, try doing a little cough, or pretend you are blowing your nose, and you should feel these muscles.

When you take your stirrups back the leathers may feel shorter, because you are sitting in a better position. You might feel that you want to let your stirrups down longer — this is fine, but it is probably best just to go down one hole lower. As your riding progresses and legs become stronger and more secure in their position you will ride longer when doing flatwork, but work towards this gradually, or you may find yourself reaching for the stirrups in trot, which will throw you out of balance. After taking your stirrups back you should feel that you are moving better with the horse, most noticeably in canter. You should also feel more secure and balanced in rising trot.

Work in a light seat

Riding in a light seat is an exercise used to help riders when they are learning to jump, but it is useful even if you never intend to do this. It helps you balance over your legs while the horse is moving, and strengthens your position and security for all aspects of riding. You will see riders in a light seat when riding cross-country; it is also the position to use when you are cantering on a hack since it makes it easier to adjust your balance as the horse travels over varying terrain. It also allows the horse to travel forward more freely, as your weight is carried off his back.

Before working in a light seat you will need to shorten your stirrup leathers a little from your flat length. Then, stand up in your stirrups and push your seat back; you should feel your heels drop lower. As you push your seat back, your upper body will come forward, although you need to make sure that you do not *lean* forward. It's a good idea to practise this in halt first and your coach can help you find the right position. As you move into your light seat you will be in a more forward position, so you will need to shorten your reins. It is easiest to ride in a light seat in trot or canter, when the horse is going forward actively. Once in a light seat you need to keep the weight into your heels and absorb the horse's movement through your knee and ankle joints. Try to keep your shoulders back and look up and forwards; if you round your shoulders or look down this will pull your weight forward. Holding this position is hard work; your legs will ache and sometimes so will your lower back, so you need to build up your strength gradually. As it develops, so will your balance and security. Start by maintaining this position for a long side of the school and then build up, practising riding 20m circles and changing the rein in this position and so on. The aim is to be able to trot and canter in a light seat, maintaining your balance and not resting your hands on the horse's neck.

A rider in a light seat in trot.

A rider in a light seat in canter.

Summary

- Before mounting, check tack for comfort and safety, girth tightness and length of stirrup leathers.

- To adjust stirrup leathers' length it's safer to keep your feet in the stirrups.

- Sitting in the correct position allows the horse to carry the rider efficiently.

- When riding in a group always ensure you leave one horse's length between you and the horse in front of you.

- If you need to stop, do this away from the track on the centre line.

- When riding independently follow the rules of the school.

- Key school figures you need to know — 20m circle, a variety of changes of rein, three-loop serpentines, figures-of-eight and shallow 5m loops.

- Work without stirrups is useful to help develop suppleness through your lower back so you can absorb the horse's movement better and be better balanced.

- Riding in a light seat will help you learn to balance over your legs when the horse is moving. It's hard work but it will develop your strength and security, keeping you safer in the saddle.

- When riding exercises over poles, ride a smooth turn on to a straight line approach, over the centre of the poles and ride straight away.

TRAINING TIPS

1. Practice makes perfect; the more riding you do the easier it gets.

2. Practise riding school figures, focusing on being as accurate as possible.

3. Watch other riders at your yard or at competitions, to pick up tips on how to use school rules, how to ride school figures, and watch how they maintain their position.

4. Watch how different horses move and the effect this has on the rider (it is interesting to watch different levels of riders riding the same horse).

5. Look in a full-length mirror to check how straight you are. Are your shoulders and hips level? Most people are naturally one-sided and you may require help from a physiotherapist to straighten you out.

6. Lunge lessons are hugely beneficial for all riders to work on balance, suppleness and position.

7. To help you develop an understanding of what the horse can feel through the reins, ask someone to hold one end of your reins while you hold the other. Keep your hands still and then ask your assistant to alter their hand position (e.g. holding the reins like handlebars, straight arms, bent elbows, increasing the pressure) to feel what happens to the contact.

8. Ride a variety of horses and compare how easy are they to sit to and how they respond to your aids. Can you ride good transitions on a lazy horse as well as a more forward-going one? If not, keep practising until you can.

What's Next?

What's Next?

We hope you have enjoyed the first volume of *Complete Horsemanship* from the BHS. If you're looking at taking this further then why not consider a career in the equine industry? A career in this industry requires hard work and determination — but the result is a very rewarding way of earning your living.

Whatever your career aspirations; caring for horses, riding professionally or coaching the next generation, there's a pathway for you. Take a look at the BHS Career Pathways:

BHS Coach in Complete Horsemanship Pathway

Career pathway	What qualifications do I need to study?				
BHS Stage 1 Complete Horsemanship	Stage 1 Care	+	Stage 1 Ride	+	—
BHS Stage 2 Complete Horsemanship	Stage 2 Care + Stage 2 Lunge	+	Stage 2 Ride	+	Stage 2 Teach
BHS Stage 3 Coach in Complete Horsemanship	Stage 3 Care + Stage 3 Lunge	+	Stage 3 Ride (Dressage) · Stage 3 Ride (Jump)	+	Stage 3 Teach
BHS Stage 4 Senior Coach in Complete Horsemanship	Stage 4 Care & Management + Stage 4 Lunge	+	Stage 4 Ride (Dressage) · Stage 4 Ride (Jump)	+	Stage 4 Teach
BHS Stage 5 Performance Coach in Complete Horsemanship	Stage 5 Care & Management + Stage 5 Lunge	+	Stage 5 Ride (Dressage) · Stage 5 Ride (Jump)	+	Stage 5 Teach
Fellow					

Please note: Complete Horsemanship pathways in dressage and jumping are available from Stage 3 onwards.

BHS Groom Pathway

Career pathway	What qualifications do I need to study?			
BHS Stage 1 Care		Stage 1 Care		
BHS Stage 2 Foundation Groom	Stage 2 Care	+	Stage 2 Lunge	
BHS Stage 3 Groom	Stage 3 Care	+	Stage 3 Lunge	
BHS Stage 4 Senior Groom	Stage 4 Care & Management	+	Stage 4 Lunge	
BHS Stage 5 Stable Manager	Stage 5 Care & Management	+	Stage 5 Lunge	

BHS Professional Rider Pathway

Career pathway	What qualifications do I need to study?			
BHS Stage 1 Ride		Stage 1 Ride		
BHS Stage 2 Foundation Rider		Stage 2 Ride		
BHS Stage 3 Rider	Stage 3 Ride (Dressage)	+	Stage 3 Ride (Jump)	
BHS Stage 4 Senior Rider	Stage 4 Ride (Dressage)	+	Stage 4 Ride (Jump)	
BHS Stage 5 Performance Rider	Stage 5 Ride (Dressage)	+	Stage 5 Ride (Jump)	

Please note: Ride pathways in dressage and jumping are available from Stage 3 onwards.

Whatever part of the horse world you would like to be involved with, qualifications and hands-on experience will enable you to get a better job, or even just understand your own horse better. Of course, a real love of horses will give you the motivation to work long hours in all sorts of weather.

The two greatest challenges for employers today are finding good workers and training them. The difference between the skills needed on the job and those possessed by applicants, sometimes called the skills-gap, is of real concern to everyone in the equine industry at every level.

Employers need reliable, responsible workers who can work out how to solve problems for themselves and who have the social skills and a willing attitude to work together with other people.

Employability skills are basic skills that are necessary to you for getting, keeping, and doing well in a job in the horse world.

Although the academic skill level required at entry-level jobs in the horse industry varies, successful employees need the ability to listen and follow instructions.

As an entry-level employee, you need to show respect for the people you work with, regardless of their background and individual differences.

You will need to see yourself as part of a team and be prepared to take the initiative to learn new things to get jobs done. It is very important that you build a good reputation for arriving at work on time, dressed appropriately, and are flexible about your working patterns when needed.

You may be looking for a job in different types of equine businesses such as stud farms, riding schools, livery yards, trekking centres or racing yards and the job description may vary depending on the type of business — but usually a groom's or stable hand's duties include the following:

- Grooming horses.

- Feeding horses.

- Mucking out stables.

- Turning horses out and bringing in.

- Tack cleaning.

- Preparing horses for lessons, treks, exercise or competitions, etc.

- General yard duties such as sweeping the yard, checking fences, etc.

As well as being physically fit, you must be willing and able to work outside in all weather conditions and be prepared to work happily with other people.

You should already have a good general knowledge and experience of horse care and stable duties.

Above all, as an equestrian worker, you should have the ability to communicate clearly with others in the industry (such as vets, grooms, employers, trainers and farriers). Working with horses can be demanding, hard work and you will need to learn to use your time efficiently.

TRAINING TIPS

Do an audit on your own skills so that you can write a job application that will stand out from the other people who may apply.

Think about drafting a CV that includes evidence of how you can demonstrate the following skills as well as your experience in the horse industry:

1. Loyalty

2. Commitment

3. Honesty

4. Enthusiasm

5. Reliability

6. Common sense

7. Ability to deal with pressure

8. Motivation

9. Flexibility

10. Working as an individual and as a member of a team

The BHS encourages you to take basic qualifications, whichever career path you choose to go down. The BHS Ride Safe, Stage 1 or 2 qualifications are the ideal way to begin your journey. You can start Ride Safe at 11 years old, Stage 1 at 14 years old, and Stage 2 at 16 years old. Stage 1 and 2 will complement other qualifications you may undertake such as Apprenticeships, Work Based Diploma (WBD or Scottish Vocational Qualifications (SVQ. Stage 1 and 2 will provide practical skills and knowledge that will prepare you well for almost any career with horses.

A recent survey reported that BHS assessments are chosen by the majority of equestrian employers.

All of the Society's Stages 1, 2 and 3 assessments have been revisited in 2017 to provide the most up to date, robust and high-quality method of exploring candidates' knowledge of riding, horse care and coaching skills, catering for every level from novice owners and beginners through to international experts.

Assessments are available at BHS Approved Centres throughout the majority of the year and are designed to be a friendly, supportive introduction to the equestrian industry.

The BHS Career Pathway team will be happy to guide you through the assessment structure. Browse our site www.bhs.org.uk/pathways, email pathways@bhs.org.uk or give the team a call on 02476 840508. Advice, guidelines and a syllabus are available for every level, so you can be confident in what you will be asked to do, and these resources will also help you make sure you are making the right choices — whatever they are.

Good luck!

To continue your journey, the
following books are also now available

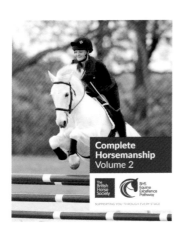 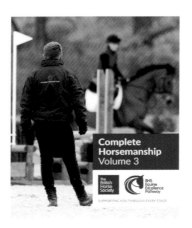 

Please see over for more information

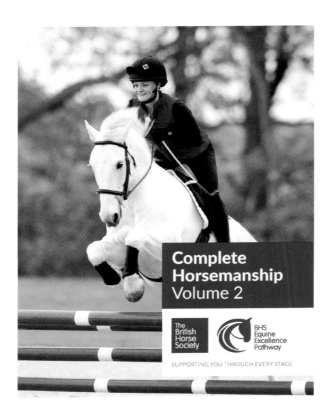

BHS Complete Horsemanship Volume 2

ISBN: 978-191001-617-6

Price: £22.50

Volume 2: Aims to develop the skills for aspiring equestrians, building on improving efficiency, depth of knowledge and understanding of equine care and management. Volume 2 introduces lungeing a horse for exercise, with practical riding skills progressing to basic jumping. Includes initial principles for teaching and coaching in the industry.

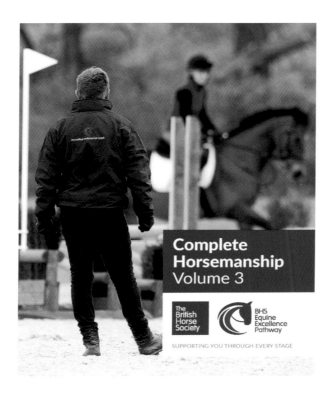

BHS Complete Horsemanship Volume 3

ISBN: 978-191001-618-3

Price: £22.50

Volume 3: An in-depth approach to developing your professional career pathway as a groom, coach or rider. Introduces the practical element of cross country jumping and considers requirements and knowledge necessary for management and care of the horse and yard.

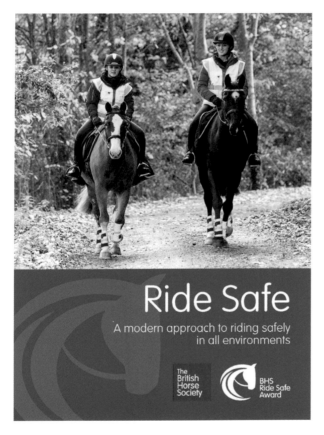

Ride Safe

A modern approach to riding safely in all environments

ISBN: 978-1-91001-626-8

Price: £8.95

PLEASE NOTE A copy of this book will be provided to anyone booking the Ride Safe Assessment* Terms and Conditions apply

A modern and revised approach to riding safely in all environments, Ride Safe is the foundation for any rider to be safe and knowledgeable when riding out in all environments including on the road, along bridleways and warming up at competitions.

Ride Safe provides a comprehensive understanding with practical examples, tips and guidance towards the Ride Safe Award assessment; ideal for all riders from occasional recreational riders to elite equestrians.

Notes

Notes

Notes

Notes

Notes